The Destiny Discovery

Find Your Soul's Path to Success

By Michelle L. Casto

Edited by Stephany Crowley & Trish Bishop
Cover art by Renee Barrett

Published by
Everyday Enlightenment International
San Antonio, Texas
USA

ISBN: 978-09674704-9-8
$14.95

Dedication:
To your beautiful Soul,
ready to be who you were born to be.

May you
discover your Destiny and
live it passionately, purposefully, and powerfully!

The Destiny Discovery
Contents

Dear Beautiful Soul,

Does your Destiny seem like a horizon that mysteriously disappears whenever you move towards it?

I have amazing news. Your Destiny is closer than you think; in fact, it's just one relationship away. This is a relationship you can have & enjoy right here, right now, should you choose to. It's a relationship you have always had but perhaps have not cultivated and nourished. It's a relationship that is essential to everything that shows up in your reality.

What is this relationship? It is the relationship with your own Soul. Many people don't think much about their Destiny, and may even be intimidated by the term, mistakenly believing that something as grand as a "Destiny" is reserved for historical figures, spiritual leaders or famous people. Well, I believe Destiny is available to everyone of us. And it is what we *choose* it to be. As you will learn, the way to connect with *your Destiny* is to follow your path with heart and to do all of the things that bring you alive.

So if your life is not working the way you would like it, take heart because you are about to embark on the journey of a lifetime; learning the exact moves that will get you where you want to go, right on time, and in tune with your inner guidance system.

We sit at the cusp of a major shift in consciousness that will forever change the landscape of life as we know it. Everyone has a part to play, especially *you* since you are reading this book—nothing happens by accident!

There are many paths you may take to fulfill your Purpose, and they all lead to one *Divine Destiny.* That is for each of us to be awakened to the truth of who we are. It may seem hard to believe just yet; that you have an amazing Destiny that is yours to claim.

Upon reading this book and doing some soul-searching, you will discover what it means for you. You can choose it to be simple or grand—it's your choice always, for even though it is there, and it is yours, it is also yours to choose—and you created that too. Simply put, your Purpose in life is to reach higher, love more, share your divine gifts, and live a happy and bliss-filled life. When you choose higher consciousness, it makes all the difference in the world, and leads to the success and happiness that you desire, which is more than you're even aware of right now.

I'll offer a fair warning that this journey is not for the faint of heart—most people go their whole lives without thinking, let alone coming to a conclusion, about the deeper questions of life such as:

Who am I?
Why am I here?
How can I help?

Congratulations on being the brave soul who is willing to go within and see yourself as the source of all that you create. Bravo! Well Done! Really, *you* are so very powerful. Starting right now, you are charting a brand new course for your life; one that is dedicated to getting to know yourself to grow into your full potential as your Soul sees it, which is infinitely more powerful and blissfully happy than you can even begin to see right now.

The book you are holding in your hands has been culled from a lifetime of research and experience assisting people from all over the world clarify their Purpose and become conscious creators. Through a divinely guided process called *The Destiny Discovery*, I'll lead you step-by-step to discover your unique path to Destiny. To receive the most benefit from this experience, I recommend getting a journal and your favorite pen. Take quiet time to read and reflect on the questions and exercises, as these are powerful methods of communicating with your Soul. As a result, you will become empowered to go where your Soul wants you to go; upgrade your social conditioning, and release anything else that blocks you from *feeling free to* BE everything you were meant to be.

Please note that words describing esoteric principles like God, Soul, and Destiny are hard to describe in human language. To appeal to as many readers as possible, I have used the words such as Higher Self, True Self, Soul, Limited Self and Ego, Soul Purpose and Destiny, God/ Spirit (and other terms), Divine Destiny and Oneness interchangeably throughout the book. I invite you to use the words that resonate for you when you come across them in the text.

By no means is this the definitive guide to Destiny, after all, Destiny is a force that is best left to the Great Mystery. Rather this book is a reminder of what you already know. See me as one of your "divine appointments" a trusted guide to help you walk your path with more clarity, confidence and purpose.

To discover your destiny is to discover the greatest 'secret' of all, that just like Dorothy in the Wizard of Oz, who had the power all along, you too, have everything you need to create the life that you want. You already have the power, insight, and knowledge inside. All it takes is to see yourself in a new light and make conscious choices, then you shall have all that your heart desires.

As you may know, reading a book changes lives, and so does writing a book. I am not the same person that I was when I began writing this over a decade ago, and I intend for you to benefit from my own transformation and experience. May *The Destiny Discovery* help you to discover the greatest treasure is within and that you do have the free will to choose to live your life on Purpose.

This is an opportunity, and the best is yet to come.

To Your Divine Destiny,
Michelle L. Casto

Part One
The Soul's Journey

The Soul's Journey

What if everything we have learned in formal education is not enough to have the life we were born to live? And, more importantly, what if we have been looking in the wrong places for the treasure that is ours to claim? Have you ever noticed that the most valuable treasure can be buried in front of you in shifting sands—invisible to your eyes...it is there but nonetheless you have to do some digging—and believing—to discover it? Together, we are going to do some digging to discover what *you need to know* and begin to look in the *only place* that you will find the treasure that you seek.

The 13th century Sufi mystic, Rumi once said,
"There is a force within you that gives you life—seek that.
In your body lies a priceless jewel—seek that.
Oh wandering Sufi (Soul)
If you are in search of the greatest treasure, don't seek outside, look within, and seek that."

Looking within is what we are about to do; fortunately, we have found each other at the perfect time because for far too long human beings have been sleep-walking through their life. And now, people just like you are awakening to realize your highest potential. Truly, the time for us to remember our Divinity is here.

Have you noticed that the most exciting times in life are when we are in "discovery", that is, when we are noticing, finding or learning something for the very first time? There is a certain thrill we feel when we catch a glimpse of the puppy that is coming home with us, or when beach combing, we find the perfect pink shell or when we learn something brand new we never knew before. When it is *Self-Discovery,* we are remembering what is meant for only us to know that lifts our spirits and guides our way. Once we open the door to Self-Discovery, it often becomes a way of life, because there is always more to discover about ourselves.

The real treasure is finding what your Soul hungers for and then honoring yourself enough to receive it. You are on a spiritual journey.... to facilitate how your human desires and inclinations can reflect the creative impulses of the Soul in the 'real world'. It becomes your unique way of moving through your life searching for your unique path rather than succumbing to the conditioning and expectations of others. When you can respond to life's circumstances, experiences and events from your Soul, you find meaning in them, especially the difficult ones.

Discovering your Destiny is a journey that begins with a close look at what inspires and moves you, and delves deep to bring to light the beauty and brilliance that you are.

Truly, your greatest gift is to be who you were born to be. You become that by embarking on a hero's journey, where you will overcome challenges, meet adversity, face your deepest fears, learn to soothe your saboteur, and confront and tame the mental monsters that live in your own mind; all in the hopes of finding the "holy grail" of your very own Destiny.

No one said it would be easy. The best things in life do require focus and attention, but rest assured; it is a journey worth taking. Interestingly, you must both *search* and *uncover* your Destiny throughout your life. Sometimes you need to do something in order to discover what you want or don't want, and other times you just need to listen for guidance. The process of deep self-discovery is what I call "dancing with Destiny." The problem is that when we fail to pay attention, instead of dancing, we tend to stumble, fall, and lose our way.

Discover the Treasure Within

Now hear this, everything you need to "get it" is in your life right this very moment. Since much of our Soul's purpose is to grow and evolve, our everyday life provides the curriculum to become individuated, that is becoming an *individual*—letting go of the good opinion of other people and charting our own course. Being a person who is individuated is a good thing, but it is *not the only thing* that matters when it comes to fulfilling your Destiny.

Once we become clear about who and what we are as an individual, then we can learn to re-connect and participate authentically in unity and Oneness. To reach that highest state of consciousness, we must start with ourselves first, by knowing who we are and why we are here.

Unfortunately, we tend to compound the matter by relying on our brain and limit ourselves by past programming, when what is required is accessing our heart's intelligence.

We falsely think we can figure everything out with our brains, and that if we just look long and hard enough, we will find the Purpose we are seeking. Consider this: the brain does not make the human—the human makes the brain by what he thinks about, focuses on, and what he allows to influence his thinking. Likewise, it is most certainly *not what happens* to you that determine your happiness—it is your response to it.

Human beings can be quite resistant to letting go of the controls, and often remain stuck in *search mode*, forgetting that we already know. And then our personality takes over and creates our life by *default*, full of disappointments and painful lessons designed to wake us up to get us back onto our path—sometimes this process is subtle and sometimes, if we ignore the signs long enough, it can be extremely traumatic. As a result, we rarely have the energy or mental discipline to transcend survival mentality to grow into spiritual maturity.

The adventure begins when you decide to go on a search for meaning, and peel back the layers of the false self, to uncover the Jewel, the true you. Your Soul is your inner treasure—excavate it. See it. Know it. Love it. Honor it.

As we become the person the Divine would have us be, and be that *boldly and authentically*, life becomes truly wonderful all on its own accord. There is very little pushing, striving or stressing. We get into the flow of our life, where things come to us with ease, and we experience a lot more fun, freedom and fulfillment.

I promise that if you choose to follow the lead of Destiny, it will do the work for you and you will meet with uncommon success and happiness. To begin your journey right now, you must first make the decision and commitment to yourself, that you want more ease, happiness and joy in your life. Know that it is possible to actually love the life you live. Know that there is a place where you belong. Know that you can be complete in every way. Know that you have a unique gift to give.

What moves you forward on your journey is bringing more awareness, presence and love to whatever you doing. You will learn how to so by consciously choosing the consciousness you want: *Victim, Victor, Vehicle, or Vessel*, as each represents the four possible lives you can live.

During our time together, you will be given the two keys that will open the doors that lead to your Destiny. The first key, found in Part I of the book, will explore the **journey of your higher consciousness** and the second key, in Part II of the book, will help you to discover your **Soul's Purpose.**

Soul Alchemy

The *Destiny Discovery Process* will teach you to become a modern-day alchemist and transform pain and struggle into a life that flows with ease and grace. The original idea of alchemy was to combine things to make something new and strong. In what I call "Soul Alchemy," you will do same thing. You'll be combining the challenges and changes in your life, to become the full embodiment of the Divine—your birthright. From there, you can create your own formula for success that combines your personal growth with your innate Soul's code to find your unique meaning and Purpose in life.

A simple three step Destiny success process is to Dream, Do, and Detach. *Dreaming* opens the doors to new possibilities; *doing* puts you in energetic alignment with having what you want, and *detaching* provides peace no matter what happens. This requires a unique brand of trust and faith with your Soul that deepens throughout your journey. The skills of self-awareness and mental mastery will also help you consciously apply the process of alchemy to all areas of your life.

If you are not following your intuition or paying attention to the signs and synchronicities in your life, it is likely due to lack of *self-awareness.* If you are not honoring your personality, talents, gifts, strengths, and values, it could be because you are listening to your saboteur instead of your *Soul.* You may be letting the louder voices of fear, doubt, and disbelief drown out the voice of faith.

A key to living a life of Destiny is to grow beyond our mindset and social conditioning to access your higher consciousness. The Soul is a source of infinite wisdom; it is your direct connection with the Divine. When we live in alignment with our Soul, we have access to the guidance that leads to our Destiny.

As your personal guide, I will do my best to help you dig deep. Let's start with the phrase "living like life is heaven on earth." This sounds like a lovely idea, but how can that really happen with so much violence and instability in the world? It may not be as unrealistic as you think. The way I see it, this is when we have a healthy mind, an open heart, and as a result, a happy, joy-filled life. Now who wouldn't want to live like that?

There are people who are *awake* and those who are going through the motions of their lives in a trance. You can usually identify those who are asleep as they look like robots going through the motions of life—eating, working, making love, and yet, when you truly *look,* a deeper presence is missing. Take thirty minutes and go to a café by yourself, just spend some time watching the people around you. They are walking around with bodies, beliefs, personalities and preferences, yet some seem fully alive and radiant while others seem to have something vital missing—a twinkle of knowing in their eye, a certain lightness of being. What is missing is an awareness of, and connection to, their own Soul.

You may wonder how you can stay happy and filled with love when you are upset or uncertain about the future? All of us have dark times, however those who are awake are able to access the light of their being and even grow through life's challenges and changes.

The darkness is when you feel lost and alone. This is known as being in the pit because you have hit rock bottom, and may be filled with negative feelings—self-loathing, depression, anger, jealousy, etc. You cannot see the light and feel separated from the Divine. You may find yourself in the darkness when you go seeking 'false treasure' in external things that leave you feeling empty.

The light is all that is good in the world—love peace, faith, happiness and wisdom. In the light, you are one with the Divine. The light allows you to see what is real in this world. The more light *you are,* the easier it is to follow your true path in life. Living in the light is a place where you are supported—all you have to do is *ask and you shall receive.*

Conscious Co-creation

A consciously co-created life is a journey of transforming the darkness of unawareness into the light of truth. We do that by coming to realize that we are not limited to our body, our past history, or our personality and that in fact, we are so much more than we can see or even perceive. We are spiritual beings having a human experience while we are also human beings having a spiritual experience. It's both. We are learning to unify our human and divine selves into a blend of higher consciousness, based in peace, love and abundance.

Have you ever wondered what your Soul looks like? If asked, how would you describe yours to others? Would you start with your body parts—arms, hair color or facial features? Would you speak of defining moments that helped you to become who you are? Or would you share your preferences in lifestyle, food, wine, travel? Is your "body suit" and "personality" what makes up your Soul or is there yet another layer?

The Soul is the Divinity within you and may be the most important discovery you ever make. It is the individualized point of consciousness that is connected to the mind of God.

James Allen in the classic book, *As a Man Thinketh said, "Of all the beautiful truths pertaining to the soul which have been restored and brought to light in this age, none is more gladdening or fruitful of divine promise and confidence than this – that man is the master of thought, the molder of character, and maker and shaper of condition, environment, and Destiny."* Like Allen, I am delighted to know that my Soul is truly wise and powerful, aren't you?

A true alchemist takes the stuff of life and sees every experience as something to grow from, and gains wisdom through the process. As Shakespeare said, *"It is not in the stars that hold our destiny but in ourselves."* The experience of day-to-day destiny often means taking our scars and making them stars, even becoming master alchemists that can skillfully transform all of life's trials and tribulations into golden thread from which to weave our higher Destiny.

The great news is that you already have all that you need to succeed—you were born with an internal Guidance Positioning System (GPS), to locate the direction of your Destiny. Your inner guidance system will send you signals when you get off path, and when you remain awake and aware enough to notice the signs, synchronicities, and connections along the way, you will find your way in perfect time.

You may read a book or meet a stranger, and they may have exactly the piece that you need to move forward.

It is more than likely that this book is a missing piece for you.

Shining Your Light

I know something special about you:

You are the light of the world.

You are a precious child of the Divine and possess amazing powers of creation and manifestation.

You are ready to shift from being a seeker of the light to being a bringer of the Light.

Re-read the above statements several times, even speak them out loud if you can, and let the truth of them sink into your Soul.

Jesus, said, *"I am the light of the world" and that "You are the Light."* This means human beings are actually light-bearers, as we possess the same divine essence that is in all of creation.

Light is powerful, and illuminates everything around it. If you have dark thoughts, you pray to see the "light." If you are in the dark and turn on the light, you are able to see. The challenge is that we often have trouble seeing and owning the light that *we are.* Without seeing our own light, it is nearly impossible to find our way to our Destiny.

Since everyone has a special light, you most definitely have one too. Some people shine with joy, others emit a ray of hope, some glow with love. Still others shine with positive energy and enthusiasm. You have an inner light that attracts people, situations and things to you. You are completely unique unto yourself. In fact, on the entire planet, there is only one light like yours.

In truth, you are one with the Source of creation and therefore you are also a creator by nature. Because Source is unlimited, you are also unlimited. In fact, anything you can imagine is yours to be, do, and have —it's all there for the creating. What if you are already doing it? Creating unconsciously, without even knowing it? If it is true that you are light, and you are one with the source of creation, then are you not also the co-creator or your own Destiny?

You may as well start using your powers to manifest what you want rather than what you don't want creating consciously rather than by default! Be the bright light you were born to be—fully turned-on, alive, and aligned with your Divinity. Practice openness and receptivity, and *let life in* including the good and not-so-good. The author of *Power vs. Force,* Dr. Hawkins says that, *"what is meant by the term 'soul' is the capacity to experience life."* We are now just beginning to realize what a gift life is and how when we give to life, we are also giving to ourselves.

This is the concept of Oneness, which is part of humanity's Destiny. In this book, we will reflect upon the personal *and* the transpersonal, individual *and* collective consciousness. To reach the Divine Destiny of Oneness, we must awaken to our Soul's Destiny of accepting our Divinity. Actually, it may not even be necessary for all of us, as experts say that only 10% of the population can shift the consciousness for *all of us.*

Higher Consciousness, Soul Purpose and Personal Transformation are essential self-mastery tools that will accelerate your journey.

Accelerating Your Journey

Higher Consciousness

Your consciousness creates your reality. At every moment, you are participating in the creation of your Destiny or you are falling into default programs. To make lasting change it is necessary to embrace everything and to see the changes, challenges, and even failures as necessary stepping stones. Admittedly, it can sometimes feel like the qualifications for Greatness are too intense for any mere mortal to bear.

Often, the so-called negative experiences that you wish you didn't have to deal with are part of your path and occur to give you an opportunity to grow into who you were born to be. Remember that everything you have in your life, the good and the not-so-good, is designed to serve your evolution. We learn through contrast and personal experience what it feels like for things to *work* or *not work.* The contrast often serves to help us see what we do want, for example, how could you know calm if there was not stress or feel the joy of feeling 'found' if you had never been lost?

The moment that you can make peace with your life story, and come to understand how you actually chose all of it, you begin to take 100% responsibility for it. Then you can focus on knowing and honoring yourself in a way that accelerates your growth exponentially.

Essential to this process is removing the mask of your false self and shining the light of your true self. Contrary to popular belief, the ego is not something "evil" that many people make it out to be. When you hear the word "ego" you may think of the common definition of someone who is full of oneself, vain, and self-centered. Another point of view is that the ego is a construct of the mind that animates fear, anxiety, anger and sorrow. We do this because we want to feel safe in the world we live in. However, the ego can be useful, especially when you are up to big things in the world. A positive spin is seeing the healthy ego as "embracing greatness openly."

Limited Self and Higher Self

For our purpose, let's agree to call it the *limited self* simply because it lives a life of limitation and protection. The ego is an invented part of you whose job is to keep you safe, help you discern what you want from what you don't want, and to distinguish and differentiate who you are from everyone else. I have never met anyone who does not have an ego-they simply express their ego differently, based on their level of consciousness.

I believe we also have a *higher self* that is connected to the Divine that provides the guidance we need to be everything we were meant to be. The higher your consciousness, the more you enhance your ability to remain in alignment with the Divine. Furthermore, we have both human and divine aspects of our selves, and *both are essential* to be effective in the world. Now, more than ever before in recorded human history, each of us has an extraordinary gift, an opportunity to give expression to Divinity on earth. I invite you to consider that playing it safe, and limiting yourself, no longer serves you.

Soul Purpose

We came in with a divine design and the further away we are from that, the more soul sick we become. When we know our purpose, we feel alive, vibrant and fulfilled. Further, life is not random, there is Purpose behind everything under the sun —literally—every insect, image, idea, and human being has been divinely designed. We can not discuss Destiny without knowing our Soul's Purpose in life. Every person born has a Purpose, including you, and it is up to *you* to assign meaning to your life. Despite popular myth, you do not have to "save the world" to be on Purpose.

Being who you really are is a source of inspiration that serves a higher purpose. For example, I have a good friend who is a hair stylist and she firmly believes by giving great hair cuts and highlights, she is also helping people to see their own beauty. Another friend is a powerful truth teller, and her contribution is to show others where they are lying to themselves. Both ways of being are important and vital.

Let's start with a simple definition of Purpose. The word "Purpose" means to have intentional results. When we are *on Purpose,* we are making a conscious effort to *be* or to *create* something. Usually what we really want seems out of reach, and "impossible." We must remember that the word "impossible" is actually "I'm (I am) possible." And you are. Your Soul's Purpose is to be the deepest expression of your unique essence (which is no small matter and a lifelong journey of discovery).

Your personality wants a 'purpose in life' and is what drives you to take what is within, bring it forth and create something in the world. It's the *thing* that you must do. The Soul desires to experience its most authentic expression, which comes by doing what you are inspired to do. The ego-mind declares, "I do it all." The Soul knows, "I attract and allow it all." Learning to work in collaboration with both aspects of who we are is important to this process.

Most people fail to realize that your brain will not help you find your Purpose, that job lies within your heart. Following your heart leads you to your unique path of happiness and success, and requires courage to do so. Authentic happiness is the end goal for the human game of life. When you are happy with yourself and life, you are on Purpose.

Once authentic happiness becomes your way of being, the choices and decisions you make to fulfill your Purpose become easier, even obvious.

Personal Transformation

Transformation starts with new thoughts and new questions, and then becomes real when we take new actions or start to choose differently. Everyday you choose transformative ways of being in your thinking, feelings, and actions, which either move you closer to your perfect life or not.

It's been said that change is inevitable, and growth is intentional., and this is quite true. We are beyond mere behavioral change when we are talking about transformation. Transformation is the realization that there is a direct connection between our psychology and the reality that is our life. It is about seeing when something is not working, choosing something brand new, and even more than that, *being who you really are* rather than being who you were *conditioned* to be.

Discontent is a sign that your Soul is unexpressed. From this point on, I invite you to pay close attention to the feelings of discontent, for it is showing you where changes are needed. That is why I always say "personal transformation is the *how-to* of Destiny."

One of your most important assignments on earth is to excavate the caverns of your inner self to uncover the jewels of your own Soul. The good news is that self-transformation, integrating ego and Soul into a life that works, is a process that can be self-initiated and self-guided. Transformation is the process of becoming conscious of the many levels from which we make choices and is a lifelong process as we continually expand into higher levels of consciousness, becoming ever-more transcended and spirit-centered.

Transformation only takes an instant, with a change of thinking, with an adoption of new ideas, such as "I am not a victim in life, I have the power to co-create my Destiny." Living a transformational life means using your heart intelligence, actively and consciously pursuing personal growth opportunities, and increasing your self-awareness. Once you have had a taste of life "transformed," you will be reluctant to ever go back to the way things were.

To begin your journey, start by noticing the feelings deep inside that are calling for your attention.

Everyday Enlightenment

Higher Consciousness guides you, Soul Purpose inspires you and Personal Transformation purifies you, so you can live your Destiny.

The Yearning Undefined

"God, or a source of divinity, put together a map for our lives. That map includes opportunities—not outcomes—but opportunities. And those opportunities are contracts [or] agreements—not that our ego or personality made, but our soul did."—Caroline Myss

The Yearning Undefined

Everyone wants to know what their ultimate Destiny in life is supposed to be; we all have an ache inside of us that longs to be a part of something greater than ourselves, and a desire to do great things. Even more, we seek to know ourselves—with *accurate self-knowledge*, we can craft a personally meaningful and satisfying life. Our Soul suffers when we are living superficially, and not reflecting deeply on what matters most to us. Especially in the modern world, there seems to be a lack of time and energy for people to "seek to find the treasure within" because we are so busy being busy. Without sufficient time to self-reflect and find meaning, we become lost in the drift of the mainstream. Some of the reasons I have uncovered that people fail to live their Destiny are:

-Accepting substitutes for happiness, such as cars, homes, beautiful things, or relationships

-Chasing opportunities versus creating on purpose,

-Resisting change,

-Denying our Divinity,

-Settling for less than our heart's desires,

-Coming to career and life path conclusions too soon (or by default) and

-Identifying with what is false in roles, relationships or bank accounts.

In other words, you are not how much money you make, or the roles that you play in life. You are much more than anything that exists in the material world, and there is a part of you that longs for your personality to dare to know and live by this awareness.

To heal the *soul ache* we feel that is caused from our disconnection from our Source of Creation, we can choose to go on a *Destiny Discovery.*

So what it is to discover one's Destiny? Let's combine these two concepts so we can be on the same page to begin with, and later you will have the opportunity to define it for yourself.

Destiny: the innate desire to actualize your greatness, live true to yourself, and the spiritual energy that reminds you that you can choose your direction and Purpose.

Discovery: to realize, learn, and possess accurate Self-Knowledge

Destiny Discovery: To possess the accurate Self-Knowledge to consciously decide to walk your unique path to Destiny and Success

Why Am I Here?

Have you ever looked up in the night sky and wondered where you fit in? Have you wondered what alignment of the stars has to happen to cause the ideal constellation of experiences required to get you headed down your true path in life? What if life is about discovering *and* creating yourself? Could it be that Destiny is *both* the potential we were born with and also what we choose to do with this potential?

It's been said that decisions determine our Destiny and I would add: Destiny determines decisions; they work together, influencing each other. It's a bit of a mystery how it all works, but for the sake of our understanding, let's look at what we do know. For starters, there seem to be opposing ideas about what Destiny is. Some say the ball is in our court, others say our fate is already written. There is Destiny the "concept" and then Destiny the "experience."

In general, when we think of "my destiny," we think that means "things that are meant to be." That is why we often feel on a deep level that we are supposed to write that book, sing that song, or dance that dance. Many times it feels as if Destiny has been with us forever, which of course, it has. Until we come into right relationship with Destiny, we are stumbling along, reacting to stimuli, and perhaps, cursing our fate.

Many experts claim that we choose all of our life experiences before we are born. Who can know for sure? My guidance tells me that we come in with a map of our potential and that it is up to us to step into it (or not). So if this is true and we have a map showing us the way—then why aren't more of us highly educated and supposedly sophisticated humans accessing more of our potential? Ah, the question of all questions.

One main reason is that our ego or limited self is afraid of the change required to align with Destiny. Our ego often has a challenge accepting our Destiny; our ego uses that 'little voice' in our heads to make us think "who am I? to be or do that?"

It's surprising how our ego can create fear within us of the very things we say we want the most—true love, wealth, a life of purpose—and yet, we often give up before we even start down the path that would get us there. We've been socialized to be afraid and to doubt our own power. And so it has been easier (and more convenient) to live a life by default, accepting whatever comes our way instead of consciously choosing who we are and what we want.

See Yourself as the Divine Sees You

When we can begin to see ourselves as the Divine sees us: beautiful, talented, whole, & holy, we begin to access the heart of our being. And as we mature into our divinity, we raise our personal vibration and begin to live a life of Destiny that involves going on an inner journey to higher consciousness and living our purpose. In collaboration with other like-minded souls and our own 'self-mastery' we are led to the success and happiness that we desire.

Life success is a team sport. That is why there are so many people on the planet, to collaborate and uplift each other's journey—we all need a little help from our friends, especially those of us who intend to live our Destiny. We may benefit from other's help most of all, because our path will be unconventional with obstacles aplenty.

One thing I know for sure, is that Destiny requires space and ingenuity. Personally, creativity is very much a part of my Destiny and inspiration flows through my entire being. As I open to become a channel, like right now, as I write this sentence, *Can you feel Destiny's presence?* I simply follow the lead of inspiration and she guides me gracefully along to where I need to be and what I am to write.

And now here you are, reading this book. Your Soul is calling you forth to do something that you have no idea how to do. Since your Destiny didn't come with a set of instructions, you may be feeling pretty lost.

When you look around for evidence that this is a wise decision, and you see very few role models, you may begin to wonder if you are just plain weird. Well, *you are weird* and in my book, that is to be commended. *Weird good*, not *"weird strange."* It is *weird* to know yourself and honor your path. In fact, the original meaning of the word *weird* is one who knows her destiny. That's right, being weird means to know what is right for you.

When you start walking the *destined for greatness path,* it is natural to feel anxious, as you are exiting out of your *comfort zone* and moving into your *courage zone.* You may even feel uncomfortable as you learn some new moves. You may feel, well, *weird* and out of your element. Guess what? Your Soul wanted you to have an adventure, so just go with it, and soon you will be dancing!

You actually do know what to do to succeed and you are uncovering that information throughout this *Destiny Discovery Process*. In truth, your life is divinely designed for you to get exactly what you need to deliver your unique expression to the world. This is the journey of your lifetime and you must consciously choose to walk it—no one can do it for you and no one knows your way better than you. The best friends and psychics in the world can only remind you of what you already know.

My intention is that this book activates your ability to remember what is in your heart, and reclaim the light within; you already have the guidance you will need to succeed and live your Destiny.

What is Destiny?

Destiny should not be confused with circumstance, coincidence, or even destination. Those are outcomes of living our Destiny. The quest for self-actualization - the fulfillment of one's unique design or purpose, cannot be reached by sitting and waiting for it; Destiny can only be reached through decision and determined action. In life, there are dreamers and doers. Doers who follow their dreams and partner with divine guidance achieve their greatest goals. Destiny comes from an integral combination of using your free will, and actively engaging with Grace and Divine will.

Each of us has a unique journey to learn our Destiny because we have to first develop an intimate relationship with our Soul. Fortunately, we are becoming clearer, more open conduits for an awakened consciousness, and this gives us insight with which to navigate our way. Let's start with some basic definitions of Destiny so we can get to know this amazing mystery. The original meaning of the word Destiny is *destinere* which means "to determine."

A common definition of Destiny is that it is a spiritual force influencing an inevitable course of events that are beyond our control, as in "Destiny brought them together." Destiny implies divine intervention....a gift, message, or chance encounter. Destiny also has a feeling of familiarity. Like when you meet soul mated friends, you often feel like, "oh, there you are—where have you been all of my life?" Actors, authors, politicians and others often admit to having an inner knowing that they felt they would be famous or had a big part to play in the world.

We can learn much about Destiny from the ancient Greeks. They knew about the three fates, known as the Moira. The Greek word *moira* literally means a part or portion, and by extension one's portion in life or Destiny. The Moira controlled the metaphorical thread of life of every mortal from birth to death. They had the respect of all the Gods, even Zeus, for their incredible power. Destiny to them was a powerful Goddess. In other words, when She is on your side, life is bound to be good.

Is Destiny My Will or Divine Will?

Still others see Destiny as "pre-destination" and believe that God determined the fate of the universe throughout all of time and space. They believe that no matter what you do or don't do, certain things are bound to happen, such as falling in love with a particular person, perhaps even at a specific time in your life, say when you are 36. When it comes to Destiny, there has long been a debate. Is it free will or Divine will? With so many definitions of it, you are left to wonder "whose will is it anyway?!"

Let's look at the options:

<u>Option 1: My Destiny is Divine Will</u>. Everything that happens is pre-ordained and written down in a book that cannot be edited. This option feels like we are giving all our power away to an invisible force outside of ourselves. It also takes us off the hook for learning a sense of personal responsibility. It denies that we are creative beings with free will to choose our direction. This just doesn't feel right.

<u>Option 2: My Destiny is My Will.</u> We may think that if "it is to be, it is up to me," and that we are the only ones that have a say in the direction of our lives. This option fails to see the interconnectedness of all life and

puts us in the unenviable position of relying on sheer willpower to make things happen. It denies that there is something greater than ourselves that loves and supports us. This just doesn't feel right.

If neither of these options will explain the big picture satisfactorily—what other option do we have?

Option 3: My Destiny is a Partnership. We are in constant communication with divine grace and our free will. We learn the choreographed moves that get us into the groove of our own heart and Soul. Your *song* is the Purpose you have been bestowed that lives in your heart and the *dance steps* are the "everyday decisions" that lead to the success and happiness that you desire. Thus, *Destiny is a co-creative partnership between you and the God of your understanding.* That is why when we hear, "With God, all things are possible," we are touched on a deep level.

Every aspect of you has an important part in the play that you are directing, writing, and starring in. So why do we often miss our Destiny entirely? The miss-steps come from our human foible of forgetting what we need to remember (that we are both human and Divine) and remembering what we need to forget (our limitations, failures, people we need forgive). We confuse ourselves by pretending that *we are not* what we really are—powerful conscious co-creators. When we remember that we are intimately related to Source, and that together, we carve our unique path in life, then we begin getting in sync. The main thing required for you to initiate this reconnection is to remember that you already know how to shine your bright light.

Look Within

There is an old story about how humans have forgotten their divine heritage. A long time ago, when human beings were about to be created, a committee of gods got together to decide where the secret of life should be placed. All the gods were in agreement that the secret should be hidden somewhere clever, so that people would have an adventure to find it. But the gods had a hard time agreeing where it would be most challenging for people to locate the treasure.

"Let's hide the secret of life at the top of the highest mountain!" one god suggested. "No, no," replied another. "People will invent airplanes and helicopters and rappelling equipment, and then everyone will be able to get to it." "Then how about at the bottom of the sea?" another god posed. "Same thing," another deity answered. "They will invent submarines and diving equipment, and that will be the end of the game."

The gods sat around, hands on chin, nearly stumped, until one god lit up. "I have it!" he exclaimed. "Let's hide the answer within each person — they'll never think to look there!" And so it has turned out. When we need to know a truth, we tend to look outside ourselves for answers, and the last place we look is in our own heart. Meanwhile, all that we could ever need to know abides at the core of our being.

I am certain there is something within you calling out to you to remember who you are in this very moment. Deep inside you know who you are, why you are here, and what is next for you. You already know that it's time to let go of the life you have known so you can begin to know and live your Destiny.

Divine Appointments

Have you noticed that dreams by their very nature lie just out of our reach; and yet most people fail to build the staircase that leads to their own version of heaven on earth? We forget that we can do it and perhaps more importantly, that we can call upon celestial help to get it done. Not only do we have support, but when we "align" ourselves with what we want, it magnetizes to us because we are a match to it.

A great question to get into instant energetic alignment: "Who do I have to be right now to align with Destiny?"

Destiny works in partnership with the people in our lives and we are given ample opportunities to connect with those who can lead us further along our path. I call these people "divine appointments." The cast of characters in our lives are perfectly prepared to assist, challenge, and sometimes torment us—all for the benefit of our Soul's evolution on the path to discovering our Destiny We all came here for a Purpose, and many of us volunteer for these roles prior to our incarnation. Some divine appointments lighten our load, and others seem just to be "button pushers."

We need both to grow into our ability to love and have compassion for each other. That is why a spiritual teacher advises you to kiss the feet of the person who troubles you the most, for he is your greatest teacher (thankfully, they ask you to do this figuratively, in your own mind – not literally). This of course is much easier said than done, as most platitudes are.

Experience Your Destiny

The experience of Destiny comes from knowing your Soul's Purpose, and being in alignment with the Divine so that you can easily discover the "treasure" that is waiting for you right here, right now. Our greatest treasure is in territories within ourselves that we avoid visiting; and that is why many of us fail to find what we are looking for in life. We must go on an inner quest to find that which we seek and those who 'push our buttons' are there as a gift, forcing us to see those things inside of ourselves we would rather not see.

Let's explore this further.....the mythologist Joseph Campbell said, *"The treasure you seek is in the cave you fear to enter."* We often fail to venture past our comfort zones to see what else is out there, or may even fail to see what is right in front of our eyes. Take a client of mine, Sarah, a young and vivacious professional, who feared true intimacy and continually attracted relationships with emotionally unavailable men.

She wanted love very much, but her limited self would not allow her the vulnerability to be with the one person in her life that could give her what she really wanted. This *treasure* showed up in a good friend but she did not recognize the signs that were all around her. She identified him as "only a friend" and even when she did see the potential that he might be the "one," she would not take the step forward to find out. Keep in mind that Destiny is continually delivering us gifts, but too often, we do not recognize them because they are not showing up in the package we are expecting to see.

When it comes to our career paths, we often miss obvious clues for what we are meant to do, it's almost as if it comes too easy, we overlook it! Thus, most human beings are *looking for themselves where they are not*—and end up in detours that look like ill-fitting jobs, out-grown relationships, and worn-out beliefs. We are so busy constructing a life around us that we never stop to consider if the life we are creating actually aligns with our heart's deepest desires. That lack of mental discipline and alignment will lead to a default life full of what we don't really want.

However, *you can align* with Destiny by choosing to live life on your terms and then receiving the guidance you need to stay true to yourself. When you access higher consciousness, you automatically move into alignment with your higher self, body, mind, and spirit and that is where you will find Destiny.

Everyday Enlightenment

The enlightened realization is that life is about knowing and honoring one's self, loving and helping others, and using our free will to decide our Destiny.

Dancing With Destiny

Living a life of Destiny involves a daily commitment to act on the promptings of your Soul and the engagement of grace to help with the fulfillment of your desires and intentions. There is a saying that GUIDANCE = God, U & I Dance. What will you say when the Divine asks you to dance and honor the life you have been given? When you accept the invitation, you embrace your own Divinity, allowing yourself to be led, and moving in directions you never even imagined. You become an inspiration to others, radiating from the inside out, and you joyfully reclaim your spiritual essence. Now that is a life worth living.

Remember to RSVP

Being called is an invitation that requires a decision, however most of us forget to RSVP! If you do hear the invitation, you can say *yes* or *no thank you.* If you don't hear the invitation, you may keep stumbling along in the dark (usually cursing because of all the things you keep bumping into that hurt!) Most of us miss out on Destiny because we refuse to learn the dance steps and follow the guidance of our Soul. In addition to not knowing the dance steps to follow, we have been trained to live in our heads.

Many of us get caught up in the *idea* of **it** and are missing the *experience* of **it** that is happening right before our eyes. Instead of living in a "conscious reality," we focus on the images in our head that we have made up about the way life is supposed to be, and when it doesn't match up, we miss the chance to discover the very treasure that is ours to claim. On the other hand, when we develop an attitude of gratitude for what we do have, then we effortlessly attract every great thing.

Destiny is a divine dance between your limited self and your higher self. And allowing your higher self to lead is key to finding success on your journey. Some other steps of Destiny's dance include upgrading our life story, knowing your Soul's Purpose, making life changes, and walking through the fires of personal transformation. At every step, we are learning to play with the energies of certainty, uncertainty, loss, gain, and the search for meaning. All of this sounds relatively easy, but without having a clear view of your higher perspective, it's easy to miss a step, and then stumble along, confused and adrift in a sea of unconsciousness.

Who Wants to Get into the Groove?

When dancing with a partner, you take a step, feel your way, then the next step, feel your way, then another step, and *suddenly* you are moving and grooving. Remember that each of us dances a little differently, so it's essential to be open to hearing the song in your Soul, and, of course, to notice *when* we are being asked to dance. As "fate" would have it, most times we are asked during times of change and challenge, and we may miss our cue. We have to learn to give up our illusionary sense of control and start to move to the beat of our heart, and learn to listen to a source of infinite knowledge that knows what is meaningful for us to experience and when.

Because Destiny is a few steps ahead of us, and knows where we are going, she will leave *clues* to help guide the way, so watch for them, or you may miss an important step. One thing we can say about dancing with Destiny is that it is dynamic. The word dynamic means *an energizing and powerful force that is changing and growing*. You can be sure you will get twirled around, spun sideways, and salsa your way to success once you get the hang of it all. Most importantly, because Destiny is attracted to confident and action-oriented people, she only dances with those people who believe in themselves and that are already on the dance floor!

Everyday Enlightenment
Destiny wants what you want from life.
In truth, you and Destiny are One.
You are partners dancing to the same song.

Self-Coaching Exercise:
Court Destiny
Take a few deep breathes and allow yourself to become deeply relaxed. Choose to believe that you have a Destiny and that it is here to dance with you. Invite your Destiny to talk with you. You may start by asking what she likes to be called. Next, ask anything that is on your mind. Refrain from over-thinking, just allow images and ideas to surface up from within and simply notice what you notice.

Ask Destiny to be your dance partner, and begin to relate to her with love and attention. Make her a part of you that you can connect with by opening your heart. Imagine in your mind's eye what your Destiny might look like, how she might think, move or act.

Make friends with Destiny. Tell Destiny how happy and grateful you are that she came into your life. Finally, write a Dear Destiny letter and be thankful for all the dreams that have already come true for you.

Answering the Call

"We must be willing to let go of the life we planned so as to have the life that is waiting for us." —Joseph Campbell

Answering the Call

Let's begin your *Destiny Discovery* by assessing where you currently are on your life path.

Self-Assessment Exercise:
Where Are You on Your Path of Purpose?
To chart a course to your Destiny, you must first know where you are, take a few moments to complete the following assessment. This will provide you with a starting point for your journey.

Directions:
Read each statement and then rate yourself on a scale of 1-4. There is no right or wrong answer, this will simply provide an awareness of where you currently are.

1: No 2: Sometimes 3: Most of the time 4: Yes

Statement	Rating
1. I wake up Monday mornings energized and excited for the week.	
2. I have a high degree of passion and enthusiasm for my work and roles in life.	
3. My spiritual foundation guides me in the way I live, love, and work.	
4. I have spent a lot of time searching my soul (through prayer, meditation, or self-reflection).	
5. I have a sense of empowerment and confidence in my life and decisions.	

6. I know and honor my core values.	
7. I can articulate in words and actions what my soul's purpose is.	
8. When considering opportunities, my purpose is my guiding light.	
9. Who I am and what I do is in alignment.	
10. I see personal development as crucial to the living of my Soul's purpose.	
11. I am aware of my KSA's (knowledge, skills, abilities) and use them frequently.	
12. I take time on a regular basis to assess where I am and where I want to go next.	
Add Your Total Score:	

Self-Assessment Results: The possible number of points is 48.

Less than 33 points: Beginner-Default Purpose
You are getting by in life, but may be feeling less than fulfilled, and more often than not, you feel stressed or disappointed with how your life is going. You may have taken a peek into your inner self occasionally, only to get dragged back into your default mode of existence. You find it challenging to make life decisions and may find yourself jumping from job to job or relationship to relationship, looking for yourself "where you are not."

34-38 points: Student-Pseudo Purpose
You may feel as if you are "hanging in there" or *doing fine* and yet, you also have a strong feeling that there is something *more* to life than this. You are not fully certain of your purpose, although you may have glimpses of being on purpose from time to time. Work is not likely

passionate or fun and you are settling for less than your heart's desires. You are driven "to do" by recognition or accolades.

39-43 points: Scholar-Personality Purpose
You have a clear understanding of what you want but you may not be fully aware of your purpose or allow it to guide your decisions in life. There is still unrealized potential within you that can easily be harnessed with the right guidance and support. You may have success with this and may experience "rising to the top of the career ladder," only to discover your ladder was resting against the wrong wall.

44-48 points: Master: Soul Purpose/Destiny
You are more than likely living at a higher rate of fulfillment, confidence and inner peace. You may want to embody your purpose and share it with others. Maybe you need to take who you are out into the world in a bigger way in the form of a business or some physical manifestation.

Based on the descriptions above, you may be surprised to find that you are not as far along as you thought. That is ok, you are exactly where you are supposed to be. To leap ahead, accept what is, and what has been. See and accept everything as being in divine order. For now, understand that you can choose to raise your consciousness at any time, from any starting point.

Journal Entry 1: I Choose Greatness

How will my life be different if I choose the path of greatness? Write this out: I (your name), am an amazing human being, destined for greatness and the best is yet to come.

The Quest for Success and Happiness
Most religions have teachings about happiness and yet happiness is quite elusive to the modern human being. As the Buddha taught, *"There is no way to happiness. Happiness is the way."* It is cosmic irony how we end up looking all over the creation for what is right under our feet and in our hearts. It's quite the human condition to remember and then forget, search but never find, and yet the one thing that we all have in common is our desire for happiness.

There is not a person on this planet, who does not wonder deeply what, who, & how they can experience the happiness that they know is possible. Happiness can include subsets of ease, peace, power, fulfillment, and so on, it is, of course, individually defined and experienced.

The Greek philosopher Aristotle said that, *"Happiness is the meaning and the purpose of life, the whole aim and end of human existence."* This quest seems to be imprinted in our biology and each of us seeks happiness in the best way we know how, even though the un-awakened do it by "default" instead of by conscious design. Understand that *you are a creator a*nd the focus of your creation is a happy life experience.

Happiness is the Purpose of your existence...and Purpose can only be found by choosing the path of happiness.

Even though you do have a guide, your Soul, you also have free will and can choose to ignore your guidance and walk another path. Your Soul will always try to steer you back onto your path and speaks to you through intuitive messages, signs, and synchronicities.

When you fail to pay attention to these first level nudges, you may then receive the "cosmic 2 x 4" in the form of significant set-backs, disappointments, accidents or even illness. Like a hero on a quest, we have to grow ourselves, expand our abilities and master the lessons that are being offered. These experiences all serve to accelerate our journey.

The best way to find our way to happiness is to "be happy." As you will learn, the expansion of consciousness that is happening is giving us the opportunity to discover the answer to *"what is happiness for me?"*

You probably have firsthand experience that happiness cannot be traveled to, worn, or consumed. Your true treasures are inside of you—they exist within you waiting to be discovered; still we look to the outside world to satisfy us. I know I did for years, decades even, looking to education, relationships, and business success to validate my personal value as a human being.

My Story

Let me share with you a bit of my own story and how I came to become intrigued by my part in the creation of my Destiny. My birth was not the kind of celebration one would hope for, my mother suffered severe post partum depression and my father was in Vietnam when I came into this world. My childhood allowed me to explore with curiosity, and as a sensitive soul, I was quite attuned with nature and the animals. I have fond memories of talking with the horses and exploring the farmlands that surrounded our neighborhood. From a young age, I was aware that we were all connected and that Earth was a great place to be. As an only child, I occupied myself with books because I felt no one seemed to pay close attention to me—at least that was my *story.* And so I compensated with seeking stimulation from both the world around me and the vast world within me. When I was a teenager, my parents divorced. My father and I became distant, as a result, I went through years of heart-ache. I then spent a good portion of my life trying to get the attention that I thought I needed to feel good about myself through romantic relationships and career advancement. I searched high and low for something to fill that empty space in my heart. I knew I was meant to feel much better than I was and that there certainly had to be more to life than what I was experiencing.

And you know what? That drive for happiness made me miserable —the more I sought it out, the more elusive it seemed to be. I am sure you know what I mean. It left me wondering if happiness is one of our core reasons for being alive, then why is there so much unhappiness and suffering in our world? My childhood put me on a lifelong quest to discover why people were unhappy and lacking a sense of purpose. Could it be that human beings have not had the spiritual knowledge to fulfill their Destiny and Purpose? Have we forgotten for far too long that we are children of the light who possess mighty powers of manifestation?

Until now humanity has been unable to truly access the greatness that is our birthright. Thankfully that is all changing. The ancient Mayans and Hopi Indians predicted this time of the "Great Awakening," that is: each and everyone one of us is being called forth to be *who we really are*, and sing the song that is in our Soul. This means your hands, mind, and heart are essential to co-creating a brand new world.

Over the course of my career, I have been in deep conversation and studied with some of the world's brightest luminaries, and have come to believe we are experiencing a personal and transpersonal initiation. On an individual level, we are being called to maintain peace and balance while accelerating our spiritual attunement. On a global scale, our entire system of living requires a radical new structure, one oriented towards

Oneness and unity. This higher understanding will allow us to treat each other with more compassion and less judgment.

What I know for sure is that we were born with the navigational tools necessary to find our way to our Destiny.

Your Divine Birthright

There are consequences to being myopic in the way we perceive our reality, seeing only "my story" and believing that it is all about me. When we do this we miss recognizing our role and the responsibility that was entrusted to us that will contribute to humanity's awakening. Allow yourself to expand your perception to see how you are an integral part of the Divine plan.

Perhaps you could exchange your idea of a judgmental God for a loving and supportive Creator and then begin the process of seeing the big picture and finding the role that was entrusted to you?

You might be wondering, "How does God fit into the equation?" Although I highly encourage you to do your own investigation, here is how I see it. There is God, the creator of All That Is who is a loving and intelligent force that wanted to experience itself in another form of expression. As a result humans, galaxies and who knows what else was created.

Since God made us, we are of God.

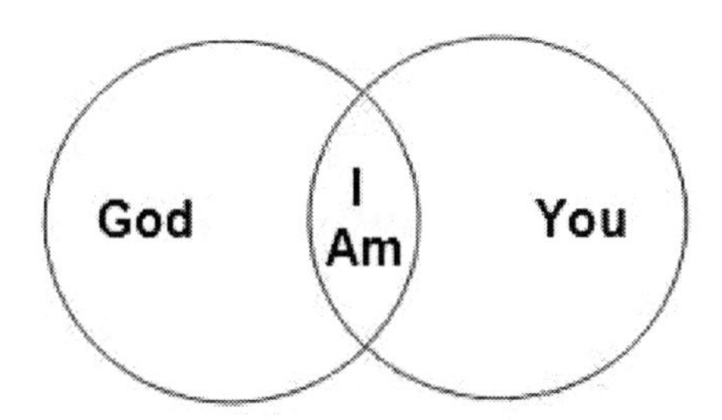

As you see in the image above, there is a sacred place where we are in unity, completely connected. I believe that when we partner with the God of our understanding that our lives work phenomenally well.

A recent release by the Associated Press out of Raleigh, North Carolina reported that most Americans are not religious but do believe in God. Why did we separate our Creator from everything that was created in the first place? Do we honestly think we can only find faith in a building? What about experiencing the divine in nature and with each other? Is it so hard to believe that we have an inner divinity that we are just now discovering?

What If?

What if the reason we continue to deny or doubt our Divinity comes from centuries of religious dogma that is lodged in our collective consciousness? Is it possible that early on in humanity's evolution, organized religion came into power, put the "fear of God into humans" and the human leaders (who undoubtedly had power and ego issues) of those institutions started to teach separation? Maybe we believed them when they said that God is outside of us and that we had better follow their rules or else. What better way to *control* the masses than to invent scary stories of eternal damnation or to lead us with the proverbial carrot stick enticing us to 'behave' if we want to get to 'heaven'?

What if instead of religion (externally guided) we choose relationship (internally guided)? Are you open to the idea that there can be heaven on earth, that this moment, your life, *right now*, can be your heaven?

Over time, humans came to believe that we had to go to an intermediary to be in contact with our own God, or worse, that we were sinners who had something terribly wrong with us. It has taken centuries for us to awaken to the truth that we are one with our Creator and that we are perfect in our imperfections.

The Shift of Consciousness we currently find ourselves in is an opportunity to correct these and other mistaken notions. The Divine is within us and because of that, we are love. We are light. We have amazing potential. And when we remember who we really are, and start to take responsibility for our lives, we can stop blaming God or any other force outside of us, and begin the journey back to *self*.

I believe there is another realm that is witnessing our emergence and cheering for us to win the race of life. And that we can certainly call upon our ancestors, angels, and guides to help us along the way. I've certainly had the experience of feeling taken care of during times of need, most notably when I was in three serious car accidents. I'll bet you have too, if you really stop to think about it.

What if Heaven is already all around us, and we don't (yet) have eyes to see it? Jesus said these very words: "*The kingdom of heaven is spread upon the earth but you do not have eyes to see it*" in the Gospel of Thomas, a recently discovered Gospel. In my view, God is too big for one gender, let alone just one religion, and God is definitely not "an old man in the sky judging us". It is interesting to note the many names that the Divine is known by; God/Allah/Jehovah/Buddha/RA, all have the AH sound, almost as if being in relationship with it brings us a sense of peace—ahhhh.

We Are Love

Even though we are an individuated aspect of our Creator, ultimately the Divine is greater and more intelligent than our limited minds can fathom. To even try to define it seems fruitless, however, we can find similarities in different theologies. Upon study, you will discover that all religions have elements of truth in them, for instance, they all teach that ***Love is what the creative force is***.

In this time of *spiritual awakening*, we are opening to the possibility that there are many paths leading to Oneness. And most importantly, the only path that matters to you is the one that will get you to where you are destined to be—living in alignment with your Destiny.

Are you willing to question some of the beliefs that you have about how all of this all works? Are you open to the possibility that God loves you unconditionally, and that an essential way you can honor the Divine is by knowing, honoring and loving *yourself?* If so, you will definitely experience more peace and empowerment on your journey.

Change Propels Destiny

What I have seen throughout decades in the personal transformation field is that until you make the changes that you know you need to make, nothing new can be created. Purpose is discovered when you embrace the changes that your Soul is calling for. For example, how can you be on Purpose if you are tied to a job you loath? You simply would not have the energy or inspiration to consider, let alone see, what else is possible. You may even be resigned to your fate, thinking that is all that you can have.

Perhaps you have felt frustrated that a certain desire has not manifested, or you feel regret or despair over past choices. Have you been searching for happiness outside of you, perhaps even changing jobs or relationships on a regular basis? The reality is that until you upgrade your consciousness, you are destined to repeat the same patterns and experiences. Take a look around you, many people are living in a trance re-creating the same reality again and again, continuing to feel unfulfilled as a result.

There is another way, and it begins with the recognition that a pattern is running your life, and then a conscious choice to move in a new direction. I have found that it is in change that we are led to find our *true path* in life. Change propels us out of our comfort zone and into our courage zone, where greatness lives.

Think about it, Destiny is not usually found in the lifestyle that you have settled for. Destiny requires you to expand and *become more* than who you have been through the processes of personal growth and making life changes. We also have the habit of living as if on a hamster wheel, going round and round with nothing ever really changing.

Wake Up From the Trance

Carl Jung said *"What we resist, persists,"* so pay close attention to the call for change when it comes. If you've ever seen the movie *Ground Hog Day* you understand what it is to be stuck in a cycle and ignoring the signs. In the movie, the main character, Phil, has to endure living the same day over and over until he learns that he must change his consciousness in order for his life to work. He learns, the hard way, that in order to have the love and success that he desires that he must shift from being narcissistic and self-important to becoming a loving and generous spirit. In the end, he gets the girl, is well-liked by his community, and succeeds in his quest towards being the person he was intended to be.

When we get caught up in mainstream thinking, we lose our sense of self. For example, most of us have been trained and educated from an early age to just follow the traditional formula for life success; "go to the right college, get a degree in something that will pay you well and give you so-called security, take a vacation every year and then you will be successful." If you are like most, you did all of that *plus* spent years in a career field where your job was all laid out, and you knew exactly what was expected of you.

You cashed a steady paycheck and tucked your dreams away. Inside you may have felt as if you were selling your Soul in exchange for money, but no one in your environment was doing it differently, so you went along with the drift of the mainstream. All the while, you knew deep down that something important was missing from your life.

Enjoy The Dance!

Instead, why not choose to enjoy the dance—and walk the path of your destiny—fulfilled, on Purpose, and grateful for *what is* as well as excited for what you are *creating*? How would your life change if you were listening and following your heart, with a sense of peace inside? It's not just possible, it's your Destiny.

Even though following the path of Destiny can be unnerving at first, as you are being asked to ignore most of what you have been taught about how life is *supposed to be,* and proceeding on a road with very few directional signposts (at least that you can see), it is most definitely worth it. Those willing to adapt and stretch themselves will succeed in the new economy and the new world and will be richly rewarded at both the personal and Soul level.

Accepting the call of your Soul and discovering what matters most to you leads to creating life on your terms. *Individuation* is a term psychologist Carl Jung referred to as the process of coming into selfhood or self-realization. Self-realization is about the integration of the light and dark aspects of your *self* (strengths and weaknesses) that you may be afraid to own, and the acceptance that all of you is good, all of you is Divine, and all of you is worthy enough (or deserves) to know and live your Purpose.

When you have individualized, you become whole, and from this place, begin to relate with yourself and life in a much more loving and conscious way.

Everyday Enlightenment

Until we awaken to learn the lessons of our life, we will continue to recreate dramas in which our ego can gain gratification via attention from an audience.

Journal Entry 2: Advancing my Soul's Journey

Take a few minutes to write responses to the following questions in your journal. Write whatever comes to you, without analyzing it or wondering if it's the 'right' answer, just write whatever comes to you, without judgment.

Where have I played a victim in my life?
Where has fear, doubt or disbelief held me back from doing what I wanted?
What actions or choices have I been resisting?
What have I merely settled for or accepted as reality?
What can I do different to advance along my journey and discover my Destiny?

Shifting to Higher Consciousness

"There's a shift happening in humanity, a shift in consciousness, happening now because it has to happen now."—Eckart Tolle

Shifting to Higher Consciousness

For some of you, the idea of a shift in consciousness is well understood, and for others, this may be an entirely new concept. Let's start with this excerpt from Marianne Williamson's 1994 book: *Illuminata* which I feel explains what is happening on our planet:

> *"The antidote for what is fundamentally wrong is the cultivation of what is fundamentally right... Ultimately, the choice to love each other is the only choice for a survivable future. ...The opening of the heart is an awesome personal politic, providing us with an internal strength greater than any worldly power. As we receive God's love and impart it to others, we are given the power to repair the world. We have begun to recognize that our individual minds create our collective realities, and we are taking more responsibility for the world by taking more seriously our individual contributions to it. Personal transformation can and does have global effects. As we go, so goes the world, for the world is us. The revolution that will save the world is ultimately a personal one."*

Science is now discovering, we (you, me, and everyone else) are all ONE energy. Therefore, when you transform yourself, the change affects all that exists, because what is in a part, is also in the whole. Further, we are undergoing an alchemical transformation of what it means to be human. Traditionally, we have held two world views: the material and mystical. And now we are moving beyond a dualistic world view to a holistic worldview where everything—light, dark, material and mystical unify and harmonize.

Many prophecies about the Shift of the Ages that is occurring have emerged from ancient traditions of the Mayans and Hopi Indians. And with this ending of a cycle comes a sense of loss, as we find our new way, while it also provides an unprecedented opportunity for massive expansion individually and collectively.

The book, *A Course in Miracles,* teaches that the welfare of the world depends on our learning. Learning *what* you might ask? Learning how to *be love,* and live a life of higher consciousness. I don't believe anyone could argue that the time for spiritual education is here. We can no longer cast a blind eye to the ills, wrongs, and general ignorance of our current reality. *It is time* for an end of the ego and the rise of the Soul. *It is time* to move beyond shallow materialism and delve deep into our unique reason for being alive. *It is time* to live our Destiny.

With the new consciousness that is being birthed on the planet, inner lights are being awakened and activated, causing humanity to grow its "angel wings." We are blessed with the very real opportunity to ascend higher up the evolutionary ladder, where we can live our greatest and best life, full of the experiences we most cherish.

The ancient philosopher, Socrates said that "*The purpose of life is the enlightenment of the soul versus the pursuit of materialism that leads to darkness.*" Since much of our history has been about the accumulation of 'things', *it is time* for us to turn within to find the only thing that will give us what we most desire, a life of meaning and Purpose.

The Age of the Soul

I refer to this time as the *Age of the Soul* where we can choose to live a more whole-hearted, intuitive, creative, and compassionate life. Living from our hearts and souls will be the result of humanity's choice to awaken to, and accept, their relationship as Divine beings. As we embrace compassion for our human foibles and also our divine gifts, we create more space for love and conscious creation. With higher awareness, we will naturally change how we pursue happiness and make that shift in orientation from our heads to our hearts.

During the Shift of Consciousness, truth will be revealed, masks will be removed, manipulations will be seen for what they are, and the reign of the ego will end. Our greatest opportunity is to stand in our true power and glory—to radiate our light for all to see, no more turning it down so others won't feel uncomfortable or holding back our power and presence out of fear of rejection or how others will react to us.

You are here and the *time is now*, so feel free to release all that is *not you*, whether that be ego identities, false purposes, material things, or past programming.

Pause for a moment to look within at your desires, dreams, aspirations, and longings.
Ask not, '*Can I do it?' Ask, 'Will I enjoy it?'*
Ask not, '*What can I get?' Ask, 'What Can I give?'*
Sit with the insights that surface for you during this process.

If we are here to love others and make ourselves happy by being who we really are and doing what fills us with joy, which sounds really easy, how could we have missed the mark for so long? One reason may be that we have been denied our Divine birthright by organized religions. If you look back at history, much of the truth about our Divinity was withheld from us. In fact, we were made to feel unworthy and that our Creator was separate from us, and, in fact, judging us and our actions. I am sure this is simply one of many reasons, however, we are fortunate to be able to choose a new reality now.

Collect the Keys to Unlock the Door to Your Destiny

I also believe that the curriculum for our enlightenment has been set by our Soul and that life is giving us the opportunities to collect the keys to our infinite wisdom. Using the key of Purpose, we can grow into our expanded self and fulfill our Divine Destiny in this lifetime.

With everything moving at an accelerated pace, as it is right now, we don't have to wait to experience being authentically happy and successful; all we have to do is choose to move into, and remain in, Divine alignment.

You have everything you need to spread your wings and fly because the Divine *you* is not something you need to create—it is something you can simply choose to remember. The Divine *you* is the light and love that you are, and your job is to clear everything blocking that truth so you can see, reclaim and shine your inner brilliance.

Embodying these rare qualities requires a new and upgraded human being, one who is in sync with their Soul's purpose and strong in loving presence. The phrase I resonate with is *a Divine Human.* And to create the peaceful and prosperous world we all know is possible requires the heart, hands and intentions of each of us to fearlessly face what is not working and collaborate to create new solutions to modern-day problems. It is no accident that you are here on Earth at this time (or the fact that you are reading this), because the Divine's plan for a new world certainly includes you.

You are at a crucial juncture where choice will determine if, how and when you show up. Will you choose to rise to your greatness or remain stagnant? Since you are reading this, then I am certain that you are ready to recognize and shine the light that you are. You can choose to awaken fully and see yourself with "real eyes"—"realize" your Divine birthright. When you see yourself as a Divine light and love-filled being with wisdom to share and gifts to offer, then you can see it in others as well.

Everyday Enlightenment

Now is the time for YOU to:

1. Reclaim your Divine inheritance.
2. Take action on your desires and dreams.
3. Shine your light.

Four Levels of Human Consciousness

You can choose to play the *Victim* in life, or you can be a *Victor*, a *Vehicle* or a *Vessel*, each represents the four possible lives you can live. The degree to which your Destiny is changing is based on your level of consciousness, that is, the focus of your *b*eliefs, *e*motions and *d*ecisions that you make from moment to moment. Today's consciousness is creating your future Destiny. In fact, when a future is predicted, it is only one of an infinite number of possibilities.

Of course, you can easily see what your predictable future is likely to be by just looking at your past events. What has happened in the past is what you are "fated" to repeat, unless, of course, you choose to upgrade your consciousness and choose the Destiny you want to experience. Psychologist Carl Jung said, *"I am not what happens to me, I am what I choose to become."* And I completely agree, the choices we make along the way help us to mature into our higher self. Think of your *Destiny Disco*very as a life-long inner journey that unfolds around two internal impulses.

1. The first impulse is the search for that something *more* that will allow you to feel whole and complete. During your journey, you will go through many false identifications — *looking for yourself where you are not*; in jobs, through your bank balance, or in the arms of lovers. What you are looking for is to know the truth about what is real and what is illusion in your own reality and to stand true in your own Truth. This is the development of your *cognition* and the ability to think for yourself.

2. The second impulse is to make powerful choices that are aligned with your True Self. It is not until you are in a *Vessel Consciousness* that you are receptive enough to make more enlightened choices. The result is that we live as either *Victims, Victors,* or *Vehicles*. It all depends on whether we fall into, or remain in, lower states of consciousness, driven by a childish need to gain attention.

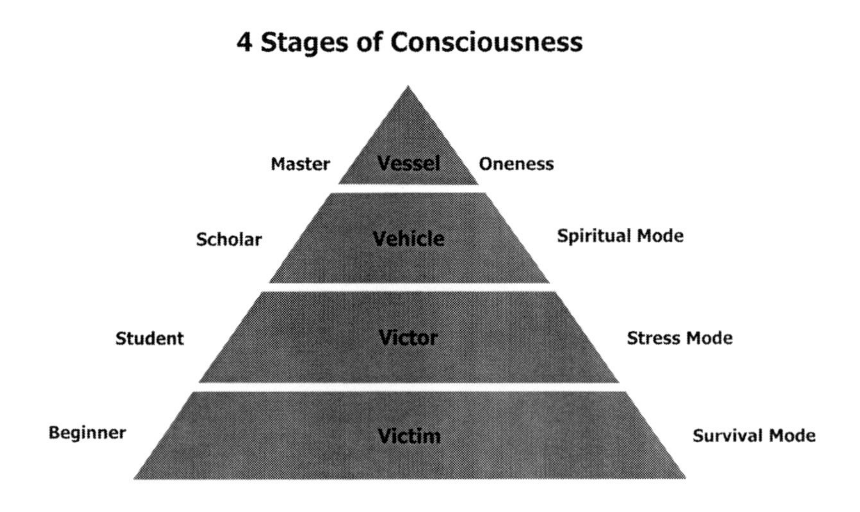

Engaging the *Destiny Discovery Process* will help you shift through four stages of consciousness during your journey.

Beginner: The life you settle for - survival mode

Student: The life you fight for – stress mode

Scholar: The life that you create - spiritual mode

Master: The life that unfolds, Your Divine Destiny - Oneness

Dorothy Gilman once said, *"It is when we make choices that we sit with the gods and design ourselves."* Let's look at your most important choice, that being which level of consciousness you will choose for yourself.

'Lower consciousness' is when you frequently resonate with fear, worry, and doubt. It is when you come from limitation. Life often feels like a "bad dream" and you are addicted to trauma and drama.

'Higher consciousness' is when you are filled with love, light, and wisdom, feeling fully connected to Source and present in the *now* moment, living with awareness and compassion.

Here is an overview of the four levels of human consciousness. Read through this list to see where you are right now. Remember to have acceptance no matter where you might be in this moment. There is no judgment necessary, no right or wrong way to be, in fact, most of us transition through these stages at different times in our life and in different circumstances.

The goal is to identify where you are most consistently so you can consciously choose a higher level of consciousness and keep moving in the forward.

Victim Consciousness: Survival Mode
Life happens *to* me

"I tend to react quickly when I feel someone has offended me."
"No matter how hard I try, I can't always get what I want."
"I don't really know who I am or why I am here."
"The life I was born into, my upbringing, tragedies and circumstances define me and make me who I am."

"I am a creature of habit, that's just the way I was made."
What now? Why me?

The victim is *waiting* for someone to rescue them or some outside circumstance to change.

When you choose *victim consciousness*, you become addicted to sad, "poor me" stories, adrenaline, and drama, and you experience mediocre results, just getting by, struggling and striving for more, constantly trying and forcing outcomes while suffering from frequent feelings of despair, depression, and frustration. Your focus as *victim* is to survive.

Victor Consciousness: Striving Mode
Life happens *by* me

"If someone gets in my way, I will push past them."
"If I want something in life, I have to be the one to make it happen."
"I struggle to keep up with bills and demands for my time."
"Just tell me what to do or what course to take and I will do it."
"You have to be assertive to get what you want from life."
"What do I need to get or do?"

The *victor* is working and studying and then working some more, believing that will get them what they want from life.

When you choose *victor consciousness*, you become addicted to winning at all costs/overcoming the odds, stress, and achieving, then you continue to experience mixed and inconsistent results, working hard to make things happen, pursuing passing desires, with only fleeting moments of happiness. Your focus as *victor* is to achieve and accumulate.

Vehicle Consciousness: Spiritual Mode
Life happens *as* me

"I know that I can get where I want to go."
"I love the process of discovering who I am and why I am here."
"I follow divine guidance."
"When I change consciousness, circumstances also change."
"There are still some things I would like to have, be, do and experience."
"Who can I assist? How can I serve?"

Although operating at a much higher consciousness than the victim or victor, the *vehicle* is still *wanting* some things to fall in place, and searching for how to allow it to happen with more ease and grace.

When you choose *vehicle consciousness*, you follow your internal guidance system. Then you experience great results on a consistent basis and attract wonderful things, people and experiences. You enjoy love, bliss, happiness, gratitude, and feelings of excitement consistently, however, you may still forget from time to time, and fall back into lower levels of consciousness. Your focus as *vehicle* is to create your ideal life.

Finally, after much personal growth and life experience, there is a momentous graduation when you shift from *Vehicle* to *Vessel* consciousness.

Vessel Consciousness: Oneness
Life happens *through* me

"The Dance dances me."
"I Am One with all that is."
"I flow with the energy of Infinite Intelligence."
"Love is what is real. Everything else is an illusion."
"I have faith that all is well and in divine order."
"Am I being the Love that I Am?"

The *vessel* is a fully Divine-realized being whose presence uplifts and heals others simply by being *who they are.*

At this highest stage of human consciousness, you realize that you are also divine in nature. You remember that you have a Purpose and came into this life to shine your personal bright light. You make the daily decision to follow Guidance; which makes *you* more divine and everything accelerates. In fact, you will receive what I like to call, *"everyday enlightenment,"* such that everything in your life serves to move you towards your Divine Destiny.

Destiny Practice:
As a vessel of the Divine, I am open to receive all the abundance the universe has in store for me.

Viva la Difference
Default Reality
Long live the difference between default reality and Destiny. The famous psychologist, Carl Jung once said, *"Until you make the unconscious conscious, it will direct your life and you will call it fate."* A simple way of stating this is that you don't know what you don't know, and so you resign yourself to what is.

Your *default reality* is the one you fell into with little deliberate intention, accepting whatever crossed your path instead of going out to find what you really wanted. I certainly know what that is like, for many years of my life, I lived in *default mode*; I settled for less than my heart's desires, accepted less than stellar in my relationships, health, wealth, and work. And then one day (after stumbling along in the dark many times which you will read about in the Awakening chapter), I awoke to the realization that "there is more to life than this" and committed myself to finding out what that was for me.

'Default living' comes from the unconscious choices you've made along the way in your relationships, career and lifestyle. It is a life that is full of struggle and stress, often known as "the school of hard knocks," because you fail to do the personal transformation necessary to learn and to *graduate* to your highest self. You are in *survival mode*; your ego makes the decisions and you may feel bored, stagnant, flat-lined, or stressed-out.

Until you upgrade your consciousness, you are destined to repeat the same patterns and experiences over and over again. As Jung states, fate could be seen as the subconscious programming that limits you.

When you let your subconscious programming guide your life decisions, you are certain to end up in dead-ends and detours that prevent you from meeting your Destiny. A key aspect of default living is doing things when your heart is just not in it. You say "*yes*" to things you ought to be saying "*no*" to. When in this state, it is like we are in a trance and have not fully awakened yet. So we stumble along, holding on to a false illusion of reality, when what we really need to do is let go.

Sage wisdom says that ignorance is identification with what is false. When we falsely identify with our roles, bank accounts, accomplishments, body, or personality, we look to outside sources to find fulfillment. This keeps us constantly searching and never looking within at the jewel that we already possess.

The main function of default living is that we are out to "get and gain", so we end up chasing opportunities and money, but never quite arriving at that state of bliss we believe we're looking for. The irony is that even when we acquire that which we seek, we still feel empty and lost.

Identify with What is True About You

If you want to graduate from *default reality*, there is a sorting out process that you must first undertake. This involves the discernment of what is *false* from what is *true* for you. Ralph Waldo Emerson wisely said, *"To be able to discern what is true is true and what is false is false; this is the mark of character and intelligence."* Be like a psychic detective who willingly tosses out dozens of false clues to find the one *right* one. Go through your life with a fine tooth comb; and see where you are being inauthentic.

Do you really need to buy a new toy, take on another committee position or join the elite country club?

We expend a great deal of precious life force energy building our "identity" from false constructs and pretense. We do this because we were never taught differently, so we unconsciously mirrored the beliefs, behaviors and conditioning of our family of origin and societal influences. Bred with a strong desire to fit in, we are willing to do just about anything to feel the love and acceptance that we have been conditioned to desire.

The False Self becomes a master at manipulation and strategy, relying on its "wits" to get what it wants. The False Self is overly concerned with what others will think, it acts from programming, and it creates a Persona to pretend to be something it is not. When we fall into the trap of trying to please others, we get entangled in roles and identities that deny who we really are.

Thus, seeing through pretense is a necessary skill in the new world, and the ability to discern real gold from the fool's gold saves you not just money, but also time and energy. Time and energy are the new money by the way; we are coming to see that our time and energy is priceless!

Recognize that where there is pretense, much has been borrowed or even imitated. Because we don't know who we really are, we look to others to model, pretending our way through life and then we wonder why we are not happy. It takes a great amount of humility to admit that you have been mistaken about who you thought you were, and it is an important first step forward towards happiness and Destiny.

Destiny

The moment you decide to be your *True Self,* and pursue your Purpose for being alive, is the moment you will be set on the path of authentic happiness.

We cannot think of Destiny without choosing the spiritual journey and knowing our Soul's Purpose. Fulfillment comes from being an 'active soul,' one who creates from their heart, no matter what you are creating. To live at this level, first give yourself permission to pursue happiness and find fulfillment in whatever way is right for you.

It's a pervasive myth that you can find happiness by listening to other people's ideas, opinions or by following the traditional formula for life success. Happiness comes when the glow and gifts that then flow from you subsequently become a benefit to others, if only from the inspiration you become for them. It comes from being an active Soul, who is sharing, loving, and contributing to the betterment of your world.

Destiny Discovery is an ongoing process, and if you want to accelerate your process, you must move out of the mainstream consensual reality. Instead of settling for less, choose to discover your Purpose, and create life on your Soul's terms. You can then re-orient your life around your purpose and experience releasing what is *not the true you*. Granted, when you step out of your default life, you will feel both exhilarated and scared because everything is so unfamiliar.

Stop Trying to Fit In. You Were Born to Stand Out.

You are truly entering a whole new territory within yourself and in the world, and may find yourself in new places, with different people. Know that feeling a little (or a lot) uncomfortable is a divine sign that you are finally on the right track, and that the initial uncertainty gives way to Destiny.

When you discover your True Self, you find everything that you are looking for! Your True Self (Soul) is eternal, infinite and directly connected to Source. The True Self desires to love, and to be, fully, everything you were meant to be.

By the way, living a life of Destiny does not mean living a perfect life—there is no such thing, perfection is in the unconditional acceptance of the imperfections. It does mean you are aligned, heart and soul, with Divine mind, that you are on Purpose, and that you are embracing more of your innate potential.

Yes, there are challenges and obstacles, but you have the capacity to learn what you need to learn. And you develop yourself well beyond the limitations of your subconscious programming. Most important, you also develop the capacity to stand on your own two feet, proud and strong in who you have chosen to become.

Everyday Enlightenment

The self you align with determines the life that shows up for you.

Destiny Practice:

I surrender my false ideas, identifications and attachments. I release the need to strive, push and do. I embrace my Divinity and ask to stay in alignment with what is true, good and holy in this world. Let me be a blessing and source of happiness to others in my life (you can list their names). And let me be happy and content with who I am, what I am, and where I am.

Who Are You Really?

The Shift of consciousness calls us to move from *me to we*, from *head to heart*, from *default reality to Destiny*. Part of this shift is the realization that we are made up of two aspects: our humanity and our divinity. The soul sees what is valuable to create and the ego implements it. An important aspect of your Divine Destiny calls you to know and embody your Divinity and to actualize your human potential. Let's look at our humanity and what it means for discovering our Destiny.

Human= Homo Sapien

We are going to start by talking about what is unique about human beings in general. First, we must know who we *are not*—we are not our personality, problems, roles, history, past, beliefs, etc. Even who we were yesterday is not who we are today, as we are either reaching towards the sunlight or dying on the vine from lack of change or challenge.

Homo Sapien is Latin for *wise or knowing man.* Human beings have a highly developed brain, capable of abstract reasoning, language, introspection, self-expression and exchange of ideas. Most importantly we have the ability to learn and to choose what we want to experience.

Human beings are transmitters and receivers of consciousness. We receive insight from our Divine connection and we also send out electromagnetic waves based on our thoughts and emotions. As mentioned, we have the opportunity to become energy alchemists where we can transmute lower vibration experiences into something higher and more useful for our growth.

However, we can also choose not to notice the spiritual realm and continue to drift along on auto-pilot. My assumption is that this will not be you, since you are still reading this!

If we *choose* to, we can learn to work with different types of energy and find our unique ways to clear, extract, balance, imprint and ground energy. This involves managing our thinking, feelings, and responses to our changes, choices, and challenges.

Human beings have a unique Purpose that is encoded within them. However, when we see our Purpose strictly from a human point of view, we get caught in the trap of focusing on *doing* our Purpose. We chase the next big thing instead of keeping the "main thing" the main thing. If what we do does not come from the heart we can get hooked by our ego which feeds off worldly recognition. Understand that Purpose is not limited to what we do, our Purpose is also to *BE* all that we were born to be and to reflect more of our inner light, presence, and power (in all that we do).

On a physical level, we were given two powerful gifts: our brain and our heart. The human brain has a neocortex that allows us to consciously execute and act. This is the "thinking" part of our human experience and the seat of our identity. When we make up our minds about something and become aligned in thought, word, and deed, we learn to direct our energy and are quite invincible. This is what makes great people great—they have mastered their own mindsets.

The Brain

A brain can be compared to a holographic projector. Imagine a movie projector with the light bulb shining through the film and creating an image on the screen. Everything that is projected on the screen becomes reality. We have conscious and unconscious movies, concepts and ideas projecting at all times.

On a quantum level, Divine intelligence knows everything and has access to all information. We can align with Divine mind and have access to more information and inspiration to guide our lives wisely. This takes quite a bit of intention and practice, but is well worth the effort.

Brains can get stuck in the mode of comparison and analysis, often neglecting to let in new insights and thoughts. We form templates of reality for our relationships, health, wealth, and then live the rest of our lives out based on early imprints, which were undoubtedly distorted. When comparison and analysis is our way of being, we spend a lot of time trying to measure up to some unrealistic standard that we set for ourselves.

Through life experiences we learn what works and does not work to get our needs met. Most of what we "learn" is how to look good to ourselves and others and in so doing we form a persona. Our *persona* is the self-identity program that runs our personality software, which is basically how we think, speak, and act when in *default mode*.

Experts say our personalities and internal programming is formed by age seven. As children we are like sponges and literally soak up thoughts and perceptions that are all around us. If you are like most, you have picked up more than a few ideas or ways of being that are not the real you.

The Heart

What about the other sacred gift, the heart? The heart has an intelligence of its own and has been said to be the seat of the Soul. Modern spiritual teachers say that our heart is the bridge to higher consciousness and that it is, in fact, more powerful and intelligent than our brain. Yet, for millennia, we have operated from our brain only, forgetting to include our heart and Soul in making our life decisions. Because of this neglect, we have suffered much.

Thank goodness we are seeking our heart intelligence to guide us now. Scientists are now discovering that our heart is able to produce and send out energy that is greater than the energy put out by our brains. They are able to measure this energy output in hertz, the same as other natural energies are measured.

From a spiritual perspective, it is reinforcing what has been said all along – that the heart, not the mind, is the key to our personal power, and it is, in fact, powerful in more ways than we have previously understood. And when we follow the path of our heart, we are led to our highest good.

We are here on earth to consciously create the life that we desire and to fulfill our mission. We do this by finding out what we do and don't want, as well as discovering our unique blessing. When our limited-self falls into ego trips, we get pulled off course; however, when we align with our Divinity, everything that is meant for us flows in effortlessly.

Limited Self: What should I do? (Controlling and anxious)
Higher Self: What would I enjoy? (Allowing and peaceful)

Soul=Light of the Divine

Although this book is not an in-depth explanation of the Soul, I want to present you will some key ideas so you can discover for yourself how to be in a closer relationship with this essential (and infinite) part of you.

Let us understand what the Soul is. As C.S. Lewis so eloquently puts it: *"You do not have a soul. You are a soul. You have a body."* The Soul is the spiritual essence within your physical form. It is eternal, unlimited, and connected to Infinite Intelligence. It knows who we are, why we are here, and where we are going.

The Greek origin for the word *psychic* means 'of the soul,' which is exactly what you want—information from your spiritual essence. Soul is the perfect expression of the Divine essence of God, the eternal aspect of you, and your Soul knows that while you are here making a HOME (heaven on mother earth), it is on a chosen mission.

The great philosopher, Plato believed that the Soul of man was eternal, pre-existent, and wholly spiritual. Many who believe in reincarnation believe that our life not only purifies the soul, but the purification comes through opportunities to learn if the Soul is willing.

Unfortunately, many people let the challenges of life bring them down rather than embracing them as the curriculum they were intended to be. They ignore these lessons for personal growth and walk through the world wounded, sending out lower vibrations. Wounds and unhealed trauma can take you away from your path of Destiny if you fall into *victim* mentality.

The irony is that when these same wounds and disappointments are seen as sacred gifts and are integrated with acceptance, they will lead you directly to your Destiny.

You Were Made to Sparkle and Shine

When you don't know your Purpose, you are still a diamond in the rough. But when you are on Purpose, you shine and sparkle in Divine radiance. The diamond is a metaphor that I use when I talk about the Soul, because of the many similarities. Have you ever heard that a diamond is nothing more than a chunk of coal who stuck to its job? When you stick through the thick and thin of your *Soul's Journey*, you see the value and meaning of your own life.

An interesting anecdote is that the origin of the word *diamond* is "adami" meaning invincible, and when you know yourself as the Divinity that you are, you too become like a diamond—invincible, beautiful, and infinitely valuable. This is important because the path to Destiny can be intimidating, so we need to know that we are capable of handling anything that comes our way.

Believing that the universe is a secure and friendly place for you provides the foundation to thrive and succeed. With this as your personal conviction, you discover a deep inner security, one that is independent of circumstances and events. Security is right there inside you, at the heart of your being. And all this time you have been looking for it where you will never find it—in the outside world.

A sense of inner security is to *absolutely know* that no one and nothing can ever really harm you. It is to *know* that no matter what curve ball life is throwing at you, that you will be taken care of and provided for. You can experience this level of knowing by being in close relationship with your Soul.

Your soul is your spiritual essence and it is best connected with in stillness, in quiet moments, often through prayer and meditation. When you practice tranquility, you will begin to receive instructions for what to do and when to do it. When we live from our Soul and follow our destined path, we naturally create a better world—because we are doing what we were born to do!

Soul-centered happiness is found in being fully present. When you are fully present, connected with your higher self, consciously guiding thoughts, feelings and behaviors, you are *being your True Self, a reflection of your Soul.* When we know this to be our true nature, our search for our identity ends— there is no longer any desire to buy things we don't really need, say things we don't really mean, or engage in any other unnecessary and inappropriate activities.

And then we give the greatest gift of all, we stop taking from life and *begin to give to life.*

The Hero's Way

"You are about to begin the hero's journey. Travel well on the quest. A life of More is your birthright. Know the vast resources that reside in you and are provided for you in the world. You have raised the battle cry of There Must Be More Than This." —Judith Wright

The Hero's Way

The archetype of the hero demonstrates how to successfully navigate through the challenges of life and shows you the most direct way to access your higher potential. The hero's journey is a Destiny you can choose to experience, however, courage is required to walk this path. The root word of courage is French for *Coeur* which means heart. Think of the cowardly lion in the movie, *The Wizard of Oz*. He had to face his fears and tap into the power of his heart to be who he was born to be, the King of the Jungle. Courage is cultivated by facing your fear and doing it anyway, and, of course, when walking the path of greatness you will have many opportunities to confront fears and doubts.

In life, you are either off-path or on-path. When you are on-path you know you are headed somewhere although you may be unsure of where exactly it will lead. If you take it step-by-step, eventually you will end up exactly where you were destined to be. How will you know the difference?

Pay attention to your feelings: when you feel frustrated and scattered, you may have veered away from your path. Off-path experiences happen by default, it is as if you fell asleep at the wheel, you feel aimless, scared, and subject to the deadly D's (dark nights, denial, doubt, depletion, delusion, delay, distractions, and detours). Life feels like a constant struggle and you seem to face one hard lesson after another as these are designed to help get you back on-path.

When you are on-path, you feel focused, fulfilled, alive, excited, relaxed, and confident, knowing that things are falling into place exactly as they are meant to, and you are effortlessly living your highest potential.

A note of caution: staying awake enough to make the daily decisions that will keep you on your true path is essential. Otherwise, you will quickly get off-path again and experience a bit more stress and delay than is necessary. Look at it like this, *all* pathways have challenges, so you may as well choose to "go for the gusto," and make your life all that it can be. Does it make sense to face difficult challenges only to end up exactly where you started? Or would you prefer to face the challenges and end up in an entirely new place, on a brand new adventure, discovering more and more of who and what you are?

Learn From Your Experiences

Your consciousness creates your reality; at every moment, you are either participating in the creation of your Destiny or falling into default programs. To make lasting change, embrace everything and see the changes, challenges, and even failures as necessary stepping stones. Admittedly, it can sometimes feel like the qualifications for Greatness are too intense for any mere mortal to bear.

Often, the so-called negative experiences that you wish you didn't have to deal with are part of your path and exist to give you an opportunity to grow into who you were born to be. Remember that everything you have in your life (the good and the not-so-good) serves your evolution. If struggle did not exist, there could be no discovery of who and what you are, why you are here and what you are capable of and that would be rather missing the point of human life.

We learn through contrast and personal experience what it feels like for things to *work* or *not work,* and it is this contrast that shows us what we do, or do not, want. After all, how could you know calm if there was not stress? The moment that you can make peace with your life story, and come to understand how you actually chose all of it, you begin to take 100% responsibility for it. Then you can focus on knowing and honoring yourself in a way that accelerates your success.

What gets and keeps you on your true path is the heroic quality of courage. You will need courage to be honest with yourself when things are no longing working and you will need courage to make changes and tough choices.

When you are off-path, you don't know who you are or you may be following someone else's advice, so you end up going in circles, *not getting where you want to be in life.* You may think "the next job or relationship" will be what I am looking for; but this is unlikely since you haven't developed a deep enough relationship with yourself.

Yes, courage is required, but there is something else you need even more—vulnerability. When you are vulnerable, you don't claim to be invincible or to "have it all together" or even to know what the heck you are doing most of the time. You bravely admit, "*I need help. I am lost. I don't how what to do and maybe even who I really am!*"

Be a Hero or Heroine in the Story of Your Life

This, to me, is the sign of the true hero, the one who admits he needs help and opens himself up to receive guidance in whatever form it is meant to come; an insight, a book, or perhaps a mentor.

See yourself as a modern-day hero— someone open to being extra-ordinary and who dares to be herself fully and completely.

-A hero (or heroine) is someone who wants an amazing life experience.

-A hero is willing to follow their guidance to that end, even when it does not make sense.

-A hero is bold enough to believe the vision in their heart for what is possible.

-A hero takes a step every day to move in their desired direction.

-A hero is someone who knows, honors, and loves herself.

-A hero bravely faces down the dragons of doubt, fear, and disbelief.

-A hero walks their chosen path with boldness and audacity.

-A hero is committed to identifying what has meaning and purpose for him and orients his life around this.

-A hero lives the greatest version of herself.

Everyday Enlightenment

Your personal achievement of Destiny is heroic and impacts others because you choose to live your Soul's Purpose in alignment with the greater divine plan for humanity.

Detours, Dark Nights, and other Deadly D's

I would love to tell you that the path to Destiny is a straight shot with very few detours or times of anxiousness, but that would not be giving you the information you need to succeed. Let's start to look at some of the pitfalls to avoid, two of the Deadly D's; detours and dark nights.

One way to tell if you are blocking your Divine Destiny is when you keep running into experiences that hurt a bit too much and then call it fate. You may even hear yourself saying "this always happens to me." Well, the reason it keeps happening is that you have not yet mastered the lesson that life is offering to you.

Remember in school you get the lesson and then take the test, but in life you get the test, and then you get the lesson!

Detours

Detours result when we fail to notice the signposts and synchronicities that are laid across our path. Detours also happen when we get entangled in unhealthy relationships or dead-end career paths. We can get out of the detours we fall into by making changes, but it often takes a lot more time, focus and energy to do so. The time it takes depends largely on how much courage you have. If you're courageous enough to see things aren't working and you are willing to take a leap of faith to make a change the timeline will be shorter than if you continue to keep your head in the sand about your level of unhappiness or un-ease.

As long as you are awake and aware of synchronicities, you will see invitations to take new roads that lead to people and opportunities that can guide you. Luckily, there are physical and symbolic signs all around. For example, when I was living in Atlanta, Georgia and was thinking of moving to Texas, I started to hear dozens of Texas related 'signs' such as license plates, conversations, songs, etc. I did make the move, as it was part of my Destiny to be Texan, but, of course, I had to choose it. When you are oblivious to the signs around you it's a bit more painful. And when you are unwilling to see what your Soul is trying to show you, you fall back into "default mode" which looks like the same experiences over and over again.

Dark Nights

What about those scary sounding "dark nights of the Soul"? Shouldn't we just avoid those at all costs? From my perspective, there are not really dark nights of the Soul, just dark nights of the ego. I say this because it is usually the ego that is putting up a fight against what is happening in reality. The process becomes more painful because it won't give up its grip and surrender to what is. Darks nights happen when we wrestle with our sense of self and re-evaluate our life path. They are something of a rite of passage and should be expected.

Because we are called to access a higher level of consciousness to align with our Destiny, there is little room for unruly egos. Instead we must listen to the wisdom of our own Soul, the whisperings of your heart's desires. Your Soul is the immortal, spiritual essence of you. Your soul carries the vibration of unconditional love, wisdom, and power and the primary source of communication is through your heart.

Observe Yourself without Judgment

When you are able to communicate with your inner self, you no longer feel that you are separate and isolated or lost, struggling to attain what you don't have. When you learn to communicate with your Soul that part of you becomes an 'observer' or 'witness' to your life, allowing you to see yourself, your choices and your actions as a third party.

Think about how easy it is to see the issues that others are struggling with, it's like there's a neon light over their head and you can see their issues as clear as day, and yet they can't see these issues for themselves. Becoming an 'observer' in your own life gives you the power to see your own 'stuff' so you can deal with it faster and more effectively than walking around with blinders on.

However, the most important reason to learn to communicate with your Soul is that your Soul has the roadmap that will lead you to your Destiny, and learning to connect with it can literally become as easy as stopping at the gas station to ask for directions.

After enough vain attempts at trying to control and manage your life, you may drop to your knees in sheer exhaustion to finally learn the power of surrender, and that is when a higher power can intervene in your plans to invite you to address your biggest fears, such as being alone, failing, or losing a lot of money.

Remember we are *partners* in this great dance called life, and Destiny wants us to have what we most want. However, we cannot act like spoiled children and expect to receive candy every time we demand it. We have to learn to cultivate patience, acceptance, and inner peace, as this is a major part of the journey of our Soul.

A client of mine experienced the power of letting go when after years of demanding a husband, she finally made peace with the fact that she *might not* meet the man of her dreams. She began to focus on loving herself more, and within three weeks of letting go of the *need* to have someone, she met a wonderful person and they began dating. It's seems we can have whatever we want, as long as we are not "needy and desperate" about it. Ever hear, "what you resist persists"?

Everyday Enlightenment

Destiny does know what you desire...just stay open and receptive to being led in your unique Dance.

Other Deadly D's

During your journey, you are bound to come across some of the other Deadly D's of Destiny, and they can stop you in your tracks. However, when properly transformed, you can channel the Deadly D energy into finding true success on your Soul's path instead. Let's look at these in more detail:

Denial: Many people live in denial instead of awareness and consciousness. It starts with denying our Divinity and then we move on to denial in other aspects of life, such as when it's time to make a life change. For example, we deny the signs that our partner is cheating on us, or we deny the signs that we are miserable at work. The way to combat denial is to be willing to change your mind about something that you thought you knew and to open your eyes to new possibilities.

Delusion: Similar to denial, delusion is a persistent set of false beliefs that will have us filter out any evidence to the contrary. There are many delusions, such as delusions of grandeur, self-importance, happiness, and deluding yourself into believing that something is working when it clearly isn't. All of these delusions keep our lives at a standstill and many times even going backwards. Radical honesty, a good look in the mirror, and facing actual results is the first step out of fantasyland and into Destiny.

Delay: Delay is putting off important tasks, decisions, actions and desired experiences in your life. It's like you put your "real life" on hold for someday. You wait and wait for someday to come, but it never does,

"Someday is not a day of the week," is a common saying. When you put your happiness or success in the future, it is always just out of reach. The way out of delay is to stop the excuses and just go for it.

Doubt: Doubts are traitors of the mind that seek to sabotage our best efforts. When we give in to doubt, we lose our clarity, confidence and personal power. To over-ride doubt's insidious power, master your mind and replace doubt with conviction.

Distraction: Distraction occurs when you get caught in the trap of an over-committed, indebted, persona-created lifestyle. We then have too much on our mind to be able to hear the still small voice inside. To become more focused, practice saying *no thank-you* and avoid getting caught up in the busyness of life.

Depletion: Depletion comes from living with the other D's while knowing there is something more you are meant to be doing. It is also created from the inability to effectively cope with modern stress. To refresh yourself, practice rejuvenating activities and work on eliminating the D's from your life.

Being aware of these Deadly D's will help you more easily succeed on your Soul's Journey.

Walking the Path of Destiny

Most fully awake and aware people (*vessels*) choose to walk the *destined for greatness* path, because they know who they are at a deep level. However, they do not pursue this path merely because it leads to so-called "greatness," rather, they walk this path out of a genuine desire to be in service to the Divine, which at some level is about being in service to self.

These people are not seeking outside of themselves for validation, they already know who they are, and so owning their greatness is a by-product of them doing what comes *naturally.* Jesus, Gandhi, Mother Theresa, Martin Luther King, Oprah, Bono, and others have shown us "the way."

Take notice of how they have shifted their point of view from "it's all about me" to "how can I be in service to others." Truly great people used to be rare, but because of the acceleration of humanity waking up, 'everyday people' like you and I are being called to be our greatness.

Mahatma Gandhi said, *"The difference between what we do and what we are capable of doing would suffice to solve most of the world's problems."* Once you begin to nurture Divinity's dream for you—with creativity, courage, enthusiasm, passion, patience, and vulnerability, you will naturally grow into your inborn talent. You may be astonished at what this divine partnership can produce. One of my friends has become famous in the art world. He has painted the likeness of people like Willie Nelson, Lance Armstrong, Dolly Parton and other modern-day lights, and yet, he never studied art. One day in his early 40's, he picked up a paintbrush, and began to paint. The result is his contribution to the healing of the world.

Model the Way-Showers

You can learn from these way-showers. Instead of resisting your illogical inclinations, go with them, see them as inspiration rather than viewing them as 'crazy'. Get out of your own way and trust that *your work* will show up how and when you are ready and that you'll know what to do.

Trust that the same power that gifted you with your potential knows how to help you bring it forth. *Trust* that this higher power wants your dreams to come true. *Trust* that *you already know* what to do to make it happen with ease. And always remember that when you are aligned, you are unstoppable.

You then begin to honor yourself and the path that is meant for you. Keep in mind that making a difference is not only about trying to save the world or being famous. In fact, leading an inspired life of purpose does not even require you to be overly altruistic, to be on every charitable board or even to put aside your own desires and dreams. You can certainly elect to do those sorts of things, if that is your true calling. What is most important, however, is that you create a life that satisfies your Soul and gives you a sense of direction and authentic happiness.

The miracle is that the way-showers have transcended their ego-based view of the world and adopted a wider, more expansive perspective that includes others. You will surely be graced with this experience to live life for more than just yourself, should you choose this path. Sometimes, you may feel not good enough or capable enough to do the work of your Soul. Do not be dismayed. Walking the path of Destiny will also give you the opportunity to heal outdated subconscious programs and patterns and align with your greatness.

One client I worked with had a past history of not being valued and felt quite intimidated by the Destiny that was calling to him to be an energy healer. We worked through the resistance and doubt that is common during the stage of *Acceptance*, and then he was able to easily move forward and start a successful business doing the work he was meant to do. The same is possible for you.

This path of Destiny is the obvious choice of the modern-day hero or heroine on a quest for success and authentic happiness—someone like *you* with the courage to consciously create life as you would love it to be.

Destiny Practice:
I honor the treasure that I am and I excitedly embark on a daily journey of self-discovery.

Part II
The Soul's Purpose

The Soul's Purpose

Think about this—everyone is searching for something to help them feel happy and joyful. If we did not each come in with a Purpose encoded within us, then what are we all searching for? It's that yearning within us that compels us to continue through the thick and thin of life's experiences.

When we know our Purpose, we have an anchor—a device of the mind and a correlating feeling, or knowing, in our heart that provides some shelter from the storms of life. When living *on Purpose* is our very way of being, we are clear that our lives have meaning, and when are off Purpose we are confused about what the point of our own life is. We may even suffer an existential crisis, such as wondering how we got on the career track we are on or wanting to make a radical move across the country to start over. On the other hand, a clearly defined Purpose provides meaning, direction, and significance, and allows you to change careers and lifestyle with consciousness and intention, so that things work beautifully.

Discovering one's Purpose is like cutting a diamond. Just like every gem-quality diamond has within it a ready-made design, waiting to be discovered, so do you. The secret is to discover and actualize your unique pattern. As a diamond needs to be excavated and polished to have worth, similarly, you have to dig deep within yourself to discover your Destiny. Just as a diamond requires friction, in order to become transparent and shine, you too need trials and tribulations to become a clear conduit for the Divine.

Soul Purpose is not a job or a career. It's not about making a lot of money, being famous, or leading a charmed life, where nothing bad ever happens. Soul Purpose is a *calling* and you are often compelled by some force inside of you. And when you follow that force, you feel happier and more fulfilled. It is about something greater than you inspiring you to create and share. It is about growing into the fullest expression that you are, and stretching beyond your comfort zone, and coming from Love.

Characteristics of a Soul Purpose

- *It Lasts a lifetime,* shaping you from birth to death, and usually doesn't change.
- *It feels bigger than you,* connecting you to others and allowing you to share your gifts with the world.
- *It supports your values,* providing you with an opportunity to excavate and bring to light your hopes, dreams, and aspirations.
- *It provides structure for what you will be and do during your lifetime,* so that you achieve maximum performance and satisfaction, experience less stress, and enjoy more meaning and authenticity.
- *It becomes the theme of your life story,* giving you more freedom to decide how to live out your personal and professional roles.
- *It is the core of where you "come from" reflected by what you say, think and do.* For example, if you are an artist, then you may see and experience your life as art itself.

When we are living in alignment with our higher Purpose, we feel more alive—filled with excitement, joy, and "contentment." We are more connected to one another as human beings and more satisfied with our chosen career path. Not being *on Purpose* leads to a constant seeking of external *things* to help you feel better about your life. When you are not *on Purpose,* you may also find yourself trying to do it all alone. You grasp at straws, basically taking anything that looks good—whether it is a new job, going back to school, moving, finding another lover—whatever fills the void of the extreme emptiness you feel inside.

Conversely, being *on Purpose* leads to an internal peace with what is unfolding in your life. You have a feeling that "all is right with the world" and you know that you have an important part to play. Also, when you are *on Purpose,* you tap into a higher power and you then receive *super*natural support. You will find the best things in life are naturally attracted to you, and that life flows along wonderfully, even abundantly.

Your Purpose is not limited to any one role, position or mission. Your purpose can be played out in many roles; for example, a significant other, daughter, friend, teacher, writer, and coach, community leader, etc. It's about coming from love and being fully present.

To reach this kind of enlightened *presence* an inner shift must first occur. When you become aware that personal transformation is necessary to living your Purpose, you have taken a big step towards your Destiny. The first step to move from *what is* into *what could be* is becoming aware of what is not working. Once you are aware of something, only then can you change it or see it differently. Making the right choices and changes are vital to living your life on purpose.

Love: The Universal Purpose

Every human being has the Universal purpose of learning how to love more openly, more fully, more completely, to love ourselves and others unconditionally. *A Course in Miracles* teaches that only love is real, and it is not about *getting* love but learning to *give love and forgiveness freely*. Unlike some misleading self-help teachings, we are not broken nor do we need to be fixed. What we do need is to BE LOVE.

Acceptance of our Divinity can be challenging for many because we were brought up to believe that God is a separate force outside of us, a parent or judge in the sky keeping tabs on when we are being good and bad, according to rules or doctrines instilled in us by our parents, religion, education and society.

Many great human beings like Jesus and Buddha have already shown us that Love is our reason for being and that through Love, everything can be transformed into a higher vibration. The great news is that every human has the ability to express his or her Divine nature to varying degrees.

Denial of our Divinity is the core reason why so many of us feel lost and aimless. Collectively, we have gotten so used to living in denial of our true nature that it leaves us feeling small and limited. Unfortunately, most people have let fear run their lives, have settled for less than their heart's desires and never taste the deliciousness of a Soul-successful life.

Some of us are just beginning to wake up from the feelings of separation to remember that we have been in connection with the Source of Creation all along. As we accept the truth of who we are—spiritual beings who are having a human experience—we can no longer live in denial. We embrace all parts of our journey, even the tough times, because when we seek understanding earnestly, we find the light that shows us our path again.

Plug In to Your True Source

New thought leader, Raymond Barker said, *"We are here to do a great work because the mind that created us knew what is wanted us to do when it created us."* I believe we were prepared in advance to do what we came to do, that we are here by design, and our gifts are fundamental to helping us become the fullest expression of that innate design.

What if you are the lamp, and Infinite Intelligence is the electricity? And what if it is your choice to plug-in or not? What if getting plugged in gives you the energy and focus you need to succeed? If you *do* want to get plugged-in, I recommend leaving mainstream thinking behind and doing your own investigation of the truth—your truth. Because when we unplug from social conditioning and plug-in to an intimate relationship with the Divine, we become inspired, filled with love and joy, we feel as if every cell in our body is on purpose, we feel 'lit'. When we are plugged in, we become the vessel, or receiving container for limitless potential, for a life that is bigger and more amazing than we can imagine.

An important reason for life on Earth is to evolve at a Soul-level while learning the spiritual lessons of love, compassion, kindness, and gratitude. Love is what we came here for and we have infinite opportunities to express love in our relationships and our work. In general, though, being on Purpose in your relationships is to help others feel good about themselves and being on Purpose in our work is about sharing our gifts with exactly the people who need to receive them in exactly the way that only we can provide them.

One area of growth for us is the work that we do. The work that contributes to the healing of the planet is directly tied to our Soul's Purpose. Many spiritual teachers believe that before you were born, a role and opportunity was entrusted to you and you alone. Before you get too caught up in trying to understand how you would heal the planet, you need to understand that this happens in various micro and macro ways. For example, the person who sings a beautiful song that is heard by even one person who then shifts their consciousness as a result of what that song meant to them has healed the planet on a micro level. The person who writes a book that touches millions of lives is healing the planet on a macro level. The person who bakes the most amazing muffins that brings joy, even for a moment, to everyone who tastes them, is healing the planet.

Live in the Present Moment

Through living our Soul's Purpose, we heal, transform and become whole by bringing our presence to the present. *Being here now* is our greatest opportunity to experience *everyday enlightenment*. Our Purpose is not to focus on the future and hope that it will be better, it is to use the energy of the present and shift it into its highest possible expression.

Also, as you learn to see the blessings of your current situation, you gain access to your power and hidden potential. When you can step back, and realize that the thing you are facing is a lesson, and that it has been orchestrated by you on a sub-conscious/Soul level, then you can learn to let go and get into the flow of where your Soul is trying to move you.

As soon as you learn to *be* in the present moment, and to accept what is, you open up to new possibilities and can easily shift from a victim to the greatest expression of *you*. You are here to love yourself and others unconditionally and it is completely up to you how you do this. A great question to ask when you are frustrated or upset is, "*What would love do?*"

Purposeful Living: Relationships and Work

John Adams once said, *"There are two educations. One should teach us how to make a living, the other how to live."* Happy relationships and fulfilling work are two of the experiences that make life worth living. When in alignment with your Purposeful path, things work out beautyfully but when you are out of alignment, things often end disastrously in both of these areas. Personal relationships and our careers are prime real estate to help you plant seeds of higher consciousness.

We want to feel successful in both our personal and professional lives, thus living a "whole" life enjoying a balance of being and doing is where the sweet spot lies. We are moving out of the dualistic paradigm of black *or* white, right *or* wrong, this *or* that., and into a holistic paradigm that allows room for *all*. In the past, you may have thought "I can either be in a great relationship *or* have a great career. I can be rich *or* happy."

When we shift into a new paradigm, we discover that *"either... or,"* is replaced by *"both...and,"* and resonates with our deepest desires. We realize that we can have it all!

Purpose is not just what is encoded within; it is also what you choose. You *can* do it all, *and* you may choose to re-focus your energy depending on the different roles you find yourself playing in life. Your professional Purpose may be put on hold for many years, as you give your time and attention to your personal Purpose, for instance, while you play the role of mother. However many people find the greatest fulfillment when they enjoy passions in both areas.

Everyday Enlightenment
Living on purpose involves an intentional act of love.
Working with purpose involves an intentional act of creation.

Purposeful Relationships

Personal Purpose focuses *on who you want to be* in relation to yourself, others, and the cosmos. When your relationships are close and supportive, you are *relating* on Purpose. When your work seems more like passionate play, you are *working* on Purpose. With Love as your over-arching *Universal Purpose,* you can't separate your *Professional Purpose* from who you are, so you will find that it often flows into your personal life; and likewise, your *Personal Purpose* flows into your professional life.

Your personal Purpose may or may not have been nurtured while you were growing up. For example, if your personal Purpose is to be giving, you may have become too giving and now struggle with being able to receive. When taken to extremes, your personal Purpose may begin to feel like a burden. You could even develop resentment and ultimately start to withhold it from others.

Carla, a fifty-five year old mother of three came to me to gain balance in her life and to heal a lifelong habit of "people-pleasing." She became aware that when she unconsciously created circumstances where she was unable to be who she really was (an empowered and strong spirit with her own needs), she would feel resentful. When she brought to light her childhood programming of putting other people's needs before her own, she then began re-creating her relationships more on Purpose, and as a result, enjoyed more balance and harmony with her friends and family.

When your Personal Purpose is kept in balance, it will be easy and enjoyable for you, and you will freely share it with others.

Purposeful Work

Confucius said, *"Choose a career you love and you will never work another day in your life."* Think about it. If we actually loved the work we were doing, work wouldn't seem so much like an obligation that brings drudgery, unhappiness and pain. How many jobs have you had that you dreaded going to? Let's look at some of the differences between a job, a career and your life's work.

A **job** is something you get paid to do and money is the primary motivation. It is easy to perform because there is not much challenge, and you will eventually find other work to do. *It may or may not fully engage you. Your Soul may or may not be present.*

A **career** is something you get paid to do that is viewed as a profession (status or identity is the motivation). It may provide more challenge, but after a while, you may get burned out, and choose to stop doing it. *It may or may not fully engage you. Again, your Soul may or may not be present.*

Your **life's work or Purpose** is something you do whether you get paid for it or not. Your Soul's need for expression is the motivation. There is plenty of challenge and personal meaning. You will always want to do it. *It definitely fully engages you and your Soul is present.*

Remember that a job can get you started toward your greater Purpose. In fact, jobs provide the very important element of exposure to different kinds of industries allowing you to discover what you do, or do not, want. Take for example, a woman who started out working in a department store as a clerk, who then moved into a management position, and finally created her life's work as an independent contractor who trains others in customer service skills. The challenge is not to get stuck at one level, unless your heart is in it of course.

Self-Coaching Exercise:
Soul at Work

To find out if your Soul is engaged in your work, place a check next to the statements that sound like you in your present work environment.

___ I am sharing my innate gifts and talents daily

___ I am doing work that is meaningful and fulfilling

___ What I do makes a positive difference in the world

___ I am standing up for something I believe in

___ I allow my Soul to lead what I do, especially when I am creating

___ Even though I am unsure of how to make everything happen, I trust that everything is unfolding in divine timing

___ I enjoy frequent moments of flow

___ I am stepping into my Greatness

___ I enjoy what I do, it feels like play

___ I have the personal freedom to do things my unique way

___ I am discovering new skills and talents that I was not aware that I had

___ I feel turned on, lit up, excited, enthusiastic

___ My work nurtures my desire to learn more, be more, do more

___ I feel fulfilled

___ I am passionate about what I do.

***The more checks you have, the more your Soul is at work.
***If you don't have many checks, then you may want to chart a new career course that allows you to express more of your True Self.

When your Soul is working, you are sharing more of who you really are, and as a result your work is performed from a level of love, higher energy, and a true sense of Purpose, which transforms everyone and everything around you. When speaking of your Purpose, it is meant to be fun; it is what you are *passionate* about. Amazingly, when you find your true Professional Purpose, it feels more like *play* because you enjoy doing it so much.

Unlike a job where there is a right and wrong way to do it, your life's work is open to interpretation and change. In fact, Purpose does not come with a set of instructions; it just shows up and you have to follow it, usually not knowing where it is headed. For instance, ask any artist if they know what to expect when they first put their paint brush on the canvas, most will say that they are compelled to create without knowing what the outcome will be. The work *guides them*—how is that for an exciting way to work!

As social structures continue to collapse, we will see the concept of work, business and commerce changing. In the new economy, everyone will be called forth to lead with heart and replace egotism with Oneness.

Everyday Enlightenment
Your Soul Purpose answers three essential questions:
Who do I want to be?
What do I want to do?
What is my unique contribution to the world?

The *Destiny Discovery* Process
In my work I have observed that there is a predictable six stage process that people experience, as they discover their Soul's Purpose, I call this *The Destiny Discovery Process.* Once you *awaken* to a new possibility, you become *aware* of the path that is calling to you, you *accept* it with your whole-heart, then you can *articulate* what it is, take *action* on it, and finally *allow* yourself to be led where the Divine wants to take you.

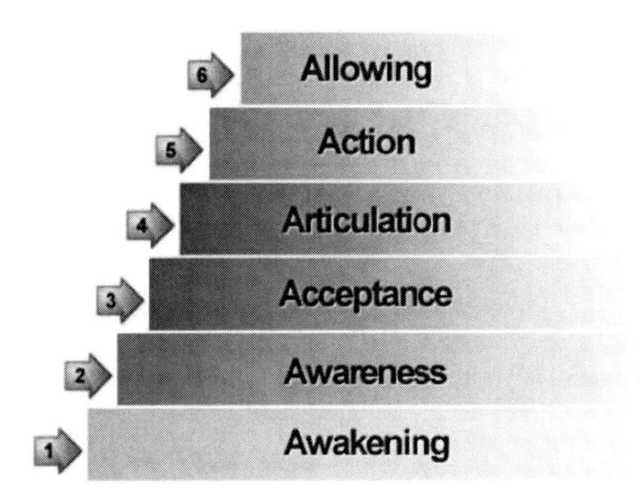

Stage One: Awakening

Awakening is the stage where you experience a dis-orienting event that causes you to ask new questions about yourself and your life, mainly to discover your unique Purpose.

When you are *Awakening*, you begin to notice a restlessness in your soul. You may have trouble sleeping or you might awaken early in the morning. You may also receive intuitive messages, or experience dreams that speak to you on a subconscious level.

Stage Two: Awareness

Awareness is the stage where you begin to pay attention to the fact that you need to find out exactly what your life is meant to be.

When you are in *Awareness*, you want to find out more about what else there is to life, you desire more fulfillment and meaning, and will often receive glimpses as to who you really are or what you are here to do. You begin to notice clues and signs everywhere, and you may even recognize that they have been there all the time, you were just unable to see them.

Stage Three: Acceptance

Acceptance is the stage where you accept who you are meant to be; your Divinity and your unique Purpose, and then come to terms with what it means to your life.

When you are in *Acceptance*, you begin to embrace the idea that your life has Purpose, and you realize it is your job to *be it* and *do it.* You agree in your heart to make it your job to find out how it is best expressed.

Stage Four: Articulation

Articulation is the stage where you articulate your life Purpose by putting it into words. It may be very simple or it could be comprehensive, but there will be a clarity that will resonate with you at the cellular level.

When you are in *Articulat*ion, you communicate what it is that you are meant to be, you share it with others, and you get excited about it and how it will manifest.

Stage Five: Action

Action is the stage where you initiate moves towards the fulfillment of your Purpose.

When you take inspired *Action*, you are allowing inspiration to lead you to big changes. You begin to make major personal and professional life choices that are more in alignment with who you are and what you are meant to do.

Stage Six: Allowance

Allowance is the stage where you live in the flow of your greatest life and become a beacon of light that uplifts others.

When you are in *Allowance*, you are open to receive the abundance that has always been yours—and you will begin to enjoy more flow, fun, freedom, and fulfillment.

As long as you are evolving and growing, you are on Purpose. However, the higher level of consciousness that you embody, the closer you are to reaching your grand Soul Purpose of enlightenment—that is knowing that you are Divine and powerful beyond measure.

Four Levels of Soul Purpose

The four levels of Purpose correspond to the four levels of consciousness: *Victim*, *Victor*, *Vehicle*, or *Vessel*. The first three levels of Purpose (default, pseudo, and personality) are what I call "false purpose traps" because they are constructed from your limited self.

When you choose these levels of self-expression, your Soul is often not fully engaged and you let fear make your decisions. When you graduate to vessel consciousness, you ARE your purpose of being Love and choosing from Love. In addition to going through the *Destiny Discovery* Process to discover your Purpose, there are four levels once you get *on Purpose*, in other words how you will live that chosen Purpose. Let me give you a real life example of how this might look. Let's say Robin's Purpose is to be a famous author—she has all the makings for it, a natural talent and a heart-felt desire. The potential is within her. She has had several major "clues" in her life that this is the right path for her. One when she was in junior high and won a writing contest. In college, she declared English as a major but then changed it to business based on advice from her family. Recently, she was let go from an administrative position that forced her to take writing more seriously.

Only Robin can decide to "graduate" from each level of reality and reach for more from life. No one is going to give her a new life on a silver platter. She has to do the inner work necessary to create a success mindset. Keep in mind, that at each level, she is serving a purpose, however, at the lower levels (default, pseudo, personality) she is not *fully expressing* herself and sharing her Divine gift(s) with the world. Obviously, the higher the level we agree to go to with our innate potential and level of consciousness, the greater the impact we have on our own lives, on others and on the world.

Default: This level reflects the relationships or jobs that you *fall into* with little conscious choice.

> *Robin works in a bookstore. It was an easy job to get and she likes being around books, but on the job, she often daydreams of being a well-known author. She ignores the calling of her heart and may not allow herself to face the discomfort and dissonance she feels inside, opting to play it safe.*

Pseudo: This level looks deceptively like you are on Purpose but your Soul is probably not engaged, and you do it more for external motivations, such as money or prestige rather than internal inspirations.

> *Robin trains to become a writing instructor. She is closer to her dream and giving more expression to her craft by helping others. She might be comfortable with this role, but deep inside she feels "inauthentic" like there is more she is meant to be doing with her talent. She wonders what it would be like to really go for it?*

Personality: This level reflects your personality and socially conditioned set of knowledge, skills, and abilities. You may even have success with it, but there is still room for more Soul. Many people mis-identify their Purpose here because they are receiving worldly recognition for what they can do.

> *Robin begins to receive accolades for her teaching and related leadership associations she belongs to. On the side, she may start writing her book, and at first, she feels fear and doubt, but eventually pushes past it. This takes a lot of courage; however, she feels like she is being more of her True Self.*

Soul Purpose/Destiny: This level brings all of who you are—body, mind, and spirit into alignment. You feel called to act, and bravely follow this path, even though you are not sure where it leads. Here you ask what life wants of you, you do work because you love to do it, and you cultivate relationships that are empowering, uplifting, and loving.

> *Robin publishes her first book to a modest level of success. She then chooses to "go for greatness" and continues to hone her writing, teaching, and now marketing skills. She has realized that teaching is also part of her path, so now she has a second source of income. The possibilities are infinite because she is living in alignment with the Divine. She has learned to trust herself and when the time comes to step forward, or even take a break; she will follow the lead of the Divine..*

By the way, there is no shame in choosing to stay at a lower level of consciousness, just realize that when you choose the higher level of consciousness, you have an amazing opportunity to accelerate the growth of your Soul. The choice is yours. You choose how to live your life and you most certainly choose the Destiny you want to experience.

What will help you choose wisely is to know if the path you are following is your True Path. Luckily, you have an innate guidance system called feelings. The two emotions that you will feel when you are headed in the right direction is that of *fulfillment,* feeling like you are bringing to realization something special into the world, and *excitement,* knowing that you are always in discovery-mode.

Six C's of True Purpose

There is a Divine plan for your life, and whenever you are feeling frustrated, confused or unfulfilled, you are not honoring some aspect of that plan. Unlike false Purposes, which are strategically constructed to gain attention or get something from the world, a True Purpose is initiated and communicated to you by your Soul.

These six C's will help you differentiate "false purposes" from your True Purpose. You can use this as a check list to confirm whether the path you are on is truly the one that leads to your Destiny.

Contract: We all come in to our life with a sacred contract and a calling that is encoded within. Our Soul knows who we are, why we are here, and how we can help ourselves and others because it created this contract before our incarnation. Our opportunity is to remember and execute this contract in our lifetime to the best of our ability.

Creativity: Creativity is what distinguishes purposeful work from other forms of work and ways of being. It goes beyond just out-of-the-box thinking, as it comes from out of this world. Our greatest gift is the creation of our chosen Destiny. When we create something, we do it from Divine love. Anything that is created from love carries a higher energy into what we are doing, and this brings healing to our world.

Clues: Living a life of Destiny involves being awake to the many clues that we are given while walking our path. When we are awake to it, we notice the signs, synchronicities, and symbols that guide our way. Think of the spiritual journey like being in a forest. You are trying to find your way, so why not follow the crumbs and trails that have been left by your higher self.

Challenge: Your Soul Purpose challenges you to move beyond your comfort zone and into your courage zone. You are stretched to learn new ways of being and skill sets that enable you to be more effective. Challenge keeps you in the game, as you are continually expanding to meet the next level required of you. The trick is to stay the course, especially when challenges arise.

Choice: Since you have free will and there is personal transformation involved in living a life of Purpose, you get to choose. Your Purpose will not just happen without all of *you* being on board. Choice gives you the freedom to step back, stay where you are, step forward, and even quantum leap ahead. Each step requires your conscious choice.

Congruency: Following your true nature enables you to be in agreement with your Purpose. Congruency is reflected when who you are, what you say, and what you do are in alignment. There is a palpable feeling of confidence and magnetism when you are congruent with your Purpose in life.

Everyday Enlightenment
You have a jewel within your Soul waiting
to be seen, expressed, and shared. Let yourself SHINE!

Journal Entry 3: Claim Your Gift

Breathe in deeply several times. Get centered in your body. Release the mental chatter as much as possible. Bring your hand to your heart. As you do, feel your heart's unique beat, savor the feeling that you are alive, and that you are unique, like no other.

As you have your hand on your heart, close your eyes (if you feel comfortable), and feeling your heart, invite your higher self to come down and connect with you.

When you feel that warm and radiant connection, ask, "What is the gift that is mine to claim?" and listen softly.

Allow visions and insights to float through you mind as you ask these questions:

Who am I being when I am my most loving?
What am I giving when I am sharing my divine gift?
If money were no concern and I knew that I could not fail, what would I do?

How can I improve my relationship with _______________?
What would I do if I were brave enough?
What is my unique blessing to share with the world?
What legacy do I wish to leave?
Then, ask anything else you would like to know.

Just relax, and soak in the insights, answers, and images that are coming from your Soul.

In the rest of the book, you will be walked through each of the *Destiny Discovery* stages in more detail so you successful navigate your journey. Remember that you have free will to choose whatever level you want to play at, and the highest level is Soul Purpose/Destiny.

Stage One: Awakening

"The millions are awake enough for physical labour; but only one in a million is awake enough for effective intellectual exertion, only one in a hundred million to a poetic or divine life. To be awake is to be alive...we must learn to reawaken and keep ourselves awake, not by mechanical aids, but by an infinite expectation of the dawn."
—Henry David Thoreau

Stage One: Awakening

Awakening is the all-important first stage in the *Destiny Discovery Process*, because without it, you will never embark on your intended Soul's journey. In fact, some people slumber through an entire lifetime and don't even realize it. There are two detours to watch for in this stage:

~ falling back asleep once you have awakened, and
~ believing that your current life plan is the *only* plan.

Most people are on auto-pilot going nowhere interesting in life, except for their contrived outings or amusements. Our ignorance of our True Self (Soul) causes us to misuse our energy and gifts, and is the basis of our physical, psychological and spiritual problems. The solution for this condition is to awaken to our Purpose and develop our spiritual gifts and powers so we can experience more of the 'good stuff' in life, such as love, happiness, health, and wealth.

You may think just because you are waking in the morning and walking around, that this means you are "awake." However, if your life isn't everything you dream of, then you might not be as awake as you think. I spent much of my life "asleep at the wheel." Even though I was pretty intelligent and into self-help, I still had my blind spots. During my pre-awakened time, I let life happen to me instead of consciously creating everything I wanted my life to be. I experienced the roller coaster ride of ups and downs, highs and lows, successes and set-backs, all the while walking in a trance instead of enjoying the dance.

This begs the question, how do we awaken when we don't even know we are asleep?! Fortunately, the Divine is always communicating to us and speaks in whatever language will likely wake us up. When we are on the wrong path it is obvious because it tends to hurt and if we are still asleep at the wheel, we can miss important signs or exits that we are supposed to take. When that happens, we stop paying close attention and may receive a wake up call from the Universe, in the form of a dis-orienting event, which could be an illness, accident, divorce, or other traumatic experience—whatever is needed to awaken you from your trance and help you get headed in a more divine direction.

Something, finally, woke me up. Actually several something's—a divorce, financial challenges, and two totaled vehicles. I should say that I woke up a little more with each event. All of this shook me to the core and woke me up to the realization that it was time to make some changes and to begin co-creating the life I wanted to live...on Purpose. It was time to burn the bridges of "safe pathways." And my life has never been the same since. Here is one incident in particular that may bring to light why you might want to choose to wake up "gently."

> On September 26, 2006 I was driving on a beautiful sunny day, doing errands and going to my bank just as I had done a thousand times before, when I made a turn from a side road onto a main road. I was hit by an oncoming car, and was unconscious. I awoke in the ambulance and asked, "Is this a bad dream?" One of the paramedics said, "No, ma'am this is not a bad dream." I was rushed to the hospital and had two CT-scans taken to be sure I had not suffered any serious damage. Miraculously, I walked out of the hospital a few hours later, and suffered not much more than a black eye. This was a strange experience for me for several reasons: What did going completely unconscious mean? Could it be that I felt a need to shut off my old system and upload a new one? It is almost as if my soul needed to upgrade my brain.
>
> The car, a gorgeous green Saab convertible was totaled. It was also the last major "thing" I was holding onto from my old life, as I was recently divorced. I intended to sell it and had just posted an ad. I was feeling a great sense of loss from not only my marriage, house, and physical things, but also the dream that went it. I was not yet awake to the deeper transformation that my Soul was calling for, and so I experienced a major accident. Keep in mind, this incident re-surfaced all the old memories of my own parent's divorce, so there was a lot of personal healing and reflection that I needed to do, which I did commence, to the best of my ability.
>
> After that close call, you would think I would have stayed awake to my Soul's call. But apparently I fell asleep again, because about six months later, I had yet another accident where I totaled the SUV that I

had purchased to replace the convertible. This time, the SUV and I ended up in the ocean. It's long story, but suffice it to say, the message was loud and clear: *"Michelle you are not in control of this trip, so let go of the wheel and get over in the passenger's seat and just enjoy the ride before you really hurt yourself or someone else."* Fortunately no one was harmed, and from this present vantage point, I can see that those many lessons were created to awaken me from my socially-induced hypnosis. What is interesting is that I had considered myself a fairly astute and aware person prior to those wrecks.

Destiny Practice:
Affirm: I choose an easy Awakening process.

Awaken Before the Nightmare

Awakening is crucial to our personal growth—hopefully yours will not be physically dangerous, but may be as emotionally draining, such as heartbreak or a wealth challenge. You will receive whatever wake-up call necessary to get your attention. Once it comes, only you will know how to interpret the messages, and just like a dream has many symbolic meanings, with various perspectives, there is an important message for you to hear. We can learn through pain or through joy, however, most of us unconsciously choose the hard way.

Everyone has a spiritual teacher—suffering. Most of us have not experienced enough pain to learn a *new way*. We have to attract "wake up calls" in order to get our little rears in gear, and move in a more Divine direction. Many people believe that a major life event must happen to put them onto a more spiritual path, and that can be the case. However, nothing tragic has to happen for you to raise your level of consciousness. Often, the whispers of your soul are what nudges you awake. I invite you to listen to your intuition early and often because it will definitely help you to experience less painful awakenings.

Everything can be used as a wake-up call, for instance, you might start with the discontent that you feel and look at what is underneath that. You could also choose to awaken by pondering questions like: *Who am I? Why am I here? What is my purpose in life?* These are some of the oldest and most important questions posed by human beings throughout history. They become even more profound when you begin to think and reflect on them for yourself.

Everyday Enlightenment

The student asked the Buddha, are you God?
Buddha said no.
The student asked Buddha, are you an angel?
Buddha said no.
The student asked then what are you?
Buddha said, I am awake.

You can be "Buddha-like" and choose to awaken (naturally) before the alarm clock goes off in the form of an accident, disappointment, break-up, or other less than pleasant wake-up call. Take it from me, waking up in an ambulance is not the way to go.

As fate would have it, humanity is receiving a massive wake-up call; your awakening will be easier and more sustainable because you will have a community to support you.

One of best self-awakening skills is that of questioning your assumptions and beliefs. Learning to ask powerful questions gives you access to new solutions, helps you make better choices, and allows you to discover new insights. Asking the right question during times of confusion or overwhelm is a very useful tool, and provides instant clarity.

For example, to discover what matters most, instead of just asking *"What Do I Want?"* also ask *"What is essential to my soul?"* Bypass your head and dive into your heart for the answers, as this is where all of what you *need to know* lives. Use a simple self-inquiry process: Take a few breaths, get centered, place a hand over your heart, ask, and then listen with an open mind.

A word about falling back to sleep; lack, limitation, and struggle are a pervasive mentality which has made it seem normal to awaken, only to drift back into default mode. I have seen so many people become excited about making life better only to fall back into old energy patterns of doubt and fear. Not fun — I know.

As a coach, I have seen clients make courageous efforts to go deeper only to get pulled back into the drift of the mainstream. It's like waking up and then falling right back to sleep again. You are certainly not alone is this quest to find what you are looking for. It's true that it does take conscious effort to stay on course in life, and I know you can do it, all because you will know the steps that lead to your Destiny.

What You Believe Becomes Your Reality

The Soul's fundamental purpose is to shape knowledge into form and create a reality that you adore. I often say, *Beliefs, Emotions, and Decisions form the basis of your reality.* Your reality is the B.E.D. you make for yourself, through what you believe, feel and do. If you want to make a bed that you love to lie in, you will want to choose consciously. *Beliefs* are thoughts you have thought so often that they form neuropathways in your brain and literally look and feel like a rut.

We get into a rut by buying into beliefs that simply are not true and then by refusing to change our minds about them. Have you ever considered that the word belief has the word *lie* in it? You see, you may have beliefs that are really just lies. The day that you start to question what you believe is a very good day.

Your *emotions* are your internal guidance system that lets you know whether you are *on-track* or *off track.* When you feel happy and light, you are following your Soul's lead. When you feel frustrated or stressed, you are relying on your own limited thinking. Your emotions also inform you when something *is* right for you and when you are barking up the wrong tree. The *decisions* you make in life either move you towards your Destiny or away from it. Since your decisions follow your emotions, which follow your beliefs, let's focus on beliefs.

Beliefs can and should be reflected upon and upgraded throughout our lifetime, unfortunately, most people still hold onto the same beliefs and paradigms they created during childhood. When you enter into the stage of *Awakening*, you become more conscious and start asking new questions that challenge long-held beliefs. A key activity in adulthood is looking at the basic beliefs that are running your life and ask: *Do these beliefs work? Do they bring me happiness? Are they serving me?* For most beliefs, the answer is *no,* primarily because you unconsciously and unknowingly adopted the belief under duress and it is no longer appropriate or in alignment with your deeper sense of self.

If your life is not working, then it is definitely time to identify your disempowering beliefs and begin to replace them with empowering ones. This is the beginning of a lifelong process of active reflection and of being more conscious of what is happening inside your own mind. Core beliefs are essentially information that we experience as coming "true" time and time again, i.e. money doesn't grow on trees, you'll never be successful without an education, etc.

Core beliefs are what "drive us" to think, feel, and act the way we do. Many times, it is not the highest reflection of who we are. However, it would be inappropriate to judge your beliefs as either good or bad, rather they should be seen as the soil from which we are now able to grow into our Soul.

We grow through asking better questions, in particular, questioning our beliefs regularly, by practicing active reflection, and above all, learning our Soul's lessons. Active reflection is the process of paying attention and bringing awareness to your internal programming. This is done through thought interruption, reflection, and conversation. There is great value in observing our internal dialogue. When we learn to upgrade behavioral patterns that do not serve our highest good and choose thoughts that are in alignment with intended outcomes, our life will not only be more purposeful, but more powerful.

Realize that to your subconscious, letting go of old beliefs is like death. And, in reality, something *is* dying; an idea or even entire paradigm. Many times, we confuse our beliefs, untrue though they may be, with our personal identity, which is why it seems scary to let them go. During this process, you may sometimes sabotage yourself as some shadowy part of you is fighting for its life. Having compassion with yourself as you surface old beliefs is a very self-honoring thing to do.

Learning to let go of limiting beliefs and shedding the skin of worn-out ways of being just might be one of the hardest dance steps to master, however, it is also the fastest way out of a default reality.

Everyday Enlightenment

Success and happiness are my birthright and come easily to me now. I live my life in total balance physically, mentally, emotionally, and spiritually. I am divinely supported and guided every step of my journey. I know that I am destined for greatness.

Knowing That You Are All That

It is very important to believe in yourself. Please do not wait for others to believe in your dreams before going for it. The way it works is if you believe, they will believe. If you are to succeed at anything, the first and most important person you must convince is *you*. Success arrives when you absolutely know you can achieve it. I invite you to go beyond just believing in yourself, and resonate your "knowing." *Know* that nothing can stop you. *Know* that you are born to succeed. *Know* with all your heart that you have what it takes. *Know* that you are being supported by the Universe.

When you think about following the path of your Destiny, you may be concerned about whether or not you will actually be successful at it. This is normal and even expected. Living a great life requires that we take a leap of faith into the great unknown to find out exactly what we are made of. My advice is to give up your deluded sense of control early on because you can never be certain if you can achieve something before you do it. Just say goodbye to uncertainty and ***Hello*** to Destiny.

You can significantly increase your chances for success by building a solid foundation of self-knowledge and seeking professional support along your way. If for some reason your path becomes too tough, you can always go back to a lower level of consciousness,. However, the greatest grief comes from *never attempting* to write that book, sing that song, or dance your dance. Consider the deep regret you would feel at the end of your life if you did not honor yourself and follow your true path.

Valuing yourself is very important, because when you can see who you are and you *value that,* you will naturally take the steps to become who you are meant to be. The ego identifies with thoughts and specializes in making comparisons, telling you that you *are not that,* to keep you playing small and limited—to avoid change. Your Soul knows that *you are all that and so much more,* (a great painter, writer, teacher, humanitarian, etc) and that not only can you *be* great, *you are great.* You just have to remove the barriers that are preventing you from being that which you already are—light and love.

You know, shining your light is the most natural thing to do in the world once you release the misperceptions that there is something wrong with you. So the next time someone asks you if you think you are God's gift to the world, smile, and say, 'Yes, I Am!'

Along with knowing how great thou are, is taking inspired action. As the *Tao* teaches, "*A journey of a thousand miles begins with the first step.*" Every small success builds more confidence that will carry you to the next step, and every step you complete not only brings you closer to the goal, but also deepens your certainty in your ability to get there. Each step, no matter how small, builds the foundation of belief that you can succeed "on Purpose." Sound simple? It is.

Consider that it may be simple, but no one said it would be easy; it takes moment to moment awareness of your innate power. You must be focused on trusting the next best inspired step to take, and then take it, knowing you are being led by the Divine.

Start your conscious awakening by letting the Universe know what level you want to play at by saying NO to the condition, situation, person, etc. that is not working. And say YES to what you do want, and know that you are worthy to receive it. When you have awakened to the true you, and you have assessed the B.E.D. (beliefs, emotions and decisions) you have made for yourself, the next thing to do is get out your magical computer and begin writing a successful life story.

Journal Entry 4: Limiting Beliefs

When thinking of knowing and living your purpose, write out 3-5 limiting beliefs you have about this area.
Choose one to focus on.
Write what doesn't work about this belief.
How does this belief make you feel?
Decide to delete this belief.
Write down what you now choose to believe.
How will you feel when you have adopted this new belief?
What will you do to reinforce this new belief?

Authoring a New Story

When something is not working in your world, there are two options: remain in the same energy and continue to create more of the same stuff—different day, or you can break-free of your past and co-create a new, much brighter future. I think you know which option to choose. You have the power to create a new life anytime you choose because your history *is not* your Destiny. Many people go their entire lives without realizing this simple, yet powerful, truth and they end up re-creating the same experiences again and again.

One of the smartest human beings that ever lived, Albert Einstein described this when he said, *"Insanity is doing the same thing over and over again and expecting different results."* Insanity does not have to be your life experience because *you now know* that there is a new way to live—with consciousness and purpose.

The story you tell yourself is the story you live. *What story will you tell to support your Destiny?* Your history is nothing but a story that you are writing. The more you identify with the negative aspects of it, the more you will remain trapped in ho-humville. Please stop telling your sad story, you are keeping yourself from living the life you were meant to live. A good way to do this is the next time you want to tell your "poor me" story, simply press "pause" and choose another line of thinking. Then keep pressing "pause" until you can finally "delete" the story. Another way to stop this habit is to repeat it to yourself or a good friend over and over again until you get sick of hearing it.

Since you are the author of your own success story, you have the power to design your life as an adventure, full of fun, ease, joy and fulfillment. It's time to let go of everything that has come before and step into your Divine Destiny. *Right now,* choose to live an inspired life. Let go of the pain of the past and move into the light of awareness, so you can move forward with ease. Start by accepting and making peace with whatever has happened in your life and forgive yourself and others who may have hurt you. See everything in your life, especially the trials and tribulations as the powerful teaching tools they were meant to be.

Many people think that when we talk of Destiny we are only speaking of the future, however it's more than that, it's the entire journey, including the past just as it was, not making yourself (or others) wrong for anything, and always forgiving yourself, acknowledging that you did your best with what you knew at the time. It all begins with simply writing a new story, complete with a happy ending.

Einstein also said that *"Imagination is greater than knowledge,"* so use the power of your imagination to act *as if* what you want is already in your realm of reality. This technique is well known for Olympic athletes, who visualize seeing themselves making the perfect shot or crossing the finish line first. Studies have shown that this is a powerful technique. Know that you are the writer, actor, and producer of your own blockbuster movie...what story do you want to tell? You can be the star of an amazing love story, a business tycoon, a world leader, or _____?

Everyday Enlightenment

You can create yourself as whoever or whatever you want to be by making a new B.E.D. (beliefs, emotions, and decisions).

Self-Coaching Exercise:
Storyboarding my life

What would it look like if your life simply worked out perfectly? *What would you be doing? Where would you be living? Who would you be with? What would you be feeling?*

Allow yourself to capture the image in your mind's eye or cut out pictures from magazines so you can visualize your dreams, and then set your intention to "live into it."

Stage Two: Awareness

"For there to be a world at all, every indigenous, natural thing must start singing its song, dancing its dance, moving and breathing according to its own nature, saying its name, manifesting simultaneously its secret spiritual signature."
—Martin Prechtel from *The Secrets of the Talking Jaguar*

Stage Two: Awareness

Awareness is the second stage in the *Destiny Discovery Process*, and where we start to see what is stopping us, as well as possible paths to pursue. There are two detours to watch for in this stage:

~ refusing to learn what the Divine is trying to teach you, and

~ being unwilling to change your mind.

When we become aware that life is stagnant and that we are missing something important, we start to see through our own self-delusions that we are "fine" and that we actually want to be *Divine.* We begin to tire of the "soul ache" we have had and seek ways to learn how to take better care of ourselves. We become aware that we have simply not owned our Divine worth, and instead we have constructed an acceptable "persona" to alleviate the pain of being separated from our Source. Of course, we can never heal this pain until we remember our own divinity.

We can then use this awareness to drop our act in favor of living with more presence and power. With awareness comes the ability to look in the mirror to see what needs to be seen. What you may see is that you are not really satisfied with mediocrity and that, in fact, you truly desire to create a new reality for yourself. Congratulations, you have just turned a very important corner on the road to your Destiny; you are electing to release your psychological patterns in favor of your Soul's Purpose.

It's not enough for us to awaken to a new possibility, we must step into it and with higher awareness, we can. Awareness is the ability to significantly increase our perspective, and to get outside of our limited self's point of view. Awareness involves thinking about our own thinking and questioning our own beliefs. It's about recognizing our feelings, and becoming *the observer* so we can get to the point where we can consciously choose them.

Awareness presents new outcomes for the many wake-up calls we will have as we walk our path. And the great news is that the more aware and responsive you become, the easier your path will be because you can see where you are *in* and *out* of alignment.

True self-knowledge is grounded in knowing your whole self.... personality and soul. At the personality level, it is important to know your preferences, values, talents, and interests. At the Soul level, it is important to be aware of what inspires you and brings you joy. In addition, becoming more faithful and less fearful can help enhance your awareness.

With faith, you believe in things that are unseen and so you move in alignment with the consciousness of the God of your understanding. You can relax and know that in the right time, all will manifest. Since the Divine's will for you is perfect happiness, if you are less than happy, then awareness is a key tool in your transformation tool box.

When life gets difficult or painful, there is likely something that is calling for our attention. I like to say that *"Life is a great teacher, for those that are teachable."* And when you see that everything serves your Purpose, you can more easily navigate your way and choose a higher consciousness, you become a Vessel. Purposeful people self-reflect—on the past, present, and future. They learn from the past, live in the present, and plan for the future, while remaining adaptable to making the changes they are called to make as living according to inspired action becomes their normal way of life. They are transformed enough to notice the psychological patterns that create their results.

Discovering your Destiny is a lot like putting a puzzle together. As you go through life, you collect different pieces of *you* from your experiences, relationships, and lessons. Through this collection of *clues*, you start to form an image of what your unique Destiny looks and feels like. The challenge comes from not being able to follow an actual visible picture, so you may become lost or get off track. Being aware gives you a chance to see the signposts along the way with more ease.

When you get stuck in a rut, and are unable to transform trials and tribulations, then you may miss the discovery that is right under your feet. However, when you choose to consciously follow the clues, when you are aware enough to see them, you find what you are looking for every time. Events guide you towards your highest good in your relationships, experiences and even your work. However, we can often miss the signposts that the Universe has posted along the way, especially when it is a particularly bumpy road.

The skills of higher awareness, reflection, and adaptation are critical to this new world. As you have seen, there are moments in our lives when we just know that we are poised on the threshold of brilliance. How we have been living, working and loving does not work anymore. You may be experiencing this revelation right now, perhaps as a divorce, job loss, bankruptcy, or health challenge, and you may be wondering how you will ever get through it.

This is your choice-point. You can see that you have created whatever circumstance you are in and have a choice to create something new or to re-create more of the same. In the awareness stage, you will move forward along your path and begin to have "Aha" moments and epiphanies, where you come to understand something you never did before. That precious moment of insight, is where you see yourself and the world in a new light.

You will no longer buy into limiting beliefs such as "I'm not good enough" or "I don't belong." You may have an epiphany like "I am great just as I am" or "I can create my life as I would like it." Most importantly, you learn to listen to your heart.

Everyday Enlightenment

Living in awareness is to attune to what is going on around you, as well as what is occurring inside of you. You become mindful of the thoughts you are thinking, your actions, and your overall relationship with yourself, others, and life itself.

Destiny Practice:

Today I choose to have crystal clear awareness about ________.

Accessing Your Heart Intelligence

You cannot figure out your Purpose with your linear, logical mind. It will keep you searching but never finding. Your Purpose is found by following the path with heart, the one that calls to you and brings you joy. While the brain leads us forward with great ideas, vision, and execution, it also has its limitations.

When left to its own devices, the brain will create all kinds of detours and traps, and actually needs the insight and wisdom of the heart. You can certainly make things happen through sheer force of will, but without balance from your heart, you are bound to create relationships and careers that only superficially satisfy your Soul. It is heart intelligence that leads us with resonance and magnetizes us to what we most desire.

You could say that "where your heart is, there lies your treasure." What our heart is drawn towards is not based upon a language or a rationale the mind can understand. Therefore, there is often a conflict between what the heart wants and what the brain 'thinks' it wants. Heart intelligence is fueled by the desire to be in relationship—in resonance—with what is important for us at a Soul level. The heart is naturally open and generous, joyous and loving, and it is one of our Purposes in life to learn how to return to our natural essence and seek wisdom there.

As Carlos Castenada brilliantly says: *"Before you embark on any path ask the question, 'Does this path have a heart?' If the answer is 'no,' you will know it and then you must choose another path. The trouble is that nobody asks the question. And when a man finally realizes that he has taken a path without a heart the path is ready to kill him. At that point very few men can stop to deliberate and leave the path. A path without a heart is never enjoyable. You have to work hard even to take it. On the other hand, a path with heart is easy. It does not make you work at liking it."*

The two confirmation questions that I have taught my clients to ask when considering any path, person, or possibility are:
Does this path have heart?
Can I give my heart to this path?

Re-framing is another powerful tool for your personal transformation toolkit. You can re-frame any experience by allowing yourself to see it from another point of view, ideally a more optimistic one. It is stopping to ask "what is the gift or lesson here?" before your emotions take you down a spiral of negativity. This skill has to be consciously chosen, however, as you may have already taken the disappointing and discouraging moments of your life personally. The moment you stop letting moments define you and choose to define them instead, is when you learn to access the wisdom of your own heart.

Finding Meaning in Your Life

I have the point of view that a life without meaning is not much of a life at all. In my coaching practice, I have worked with people on the brink of "losing it" and wanting to give up on various levels—from quitting a job they could not bear, to wrestling with understanding the challenges of their life. After all, if you cannot find meaning in your life, *what point is there for living?*

To have our existence matter, our deepest needs met, and achieve the goals we set for ourselves is an instinctive calling. Cultures throughout history have long expressed themselves through art, politics, love, and labor. The call to *be* and *do* is primal. We are creators at heart and need to feel that what we create makes a difference. In the modern world that innate urge to exist, to matter, to have meaning, often gets covered over with substitutes for happiness, and we end up getting stuck in roles, goals and environments that drain the very life from us.

Pain and suffering are often the impetus we need to seek deeper meaning in our life and to begin our *Destiny Discovery*. This is the "inner alchemy" of the Soul—the alchemical process of self-transformation, turning trials and tears into something useful for our personal growth. A personal empowerment teacher publicly admitted that she had considered suicide as a way of ending the pain of having no meaning in life. Thankfully, she was able to turn her dark night into a profitable business, and now helps others turn their pain into Purpose.

I recently read a friends 'status update' on Facebook that said, "Even with all the money, sex, and power, an unexamined life still sucks." As a society, times are changing and values are shifting—we are beginning to realize that material pursuits alone will not bring us the satisfaction that we long for in our hearts. It takes something much more, in fact, it takes becoming *someone more* to find the meaning that makes life worth living.

Believe it or not, everything in your life serves a higher Purpose, especially the tears and trials. An inspiring example of this is my client, Sally. She was shot by an ex-boyfriend and lost use of her left eye, and while his choice was to exit this plane of existence, she is choosing to "see" the meaning behind it all. Thankfully, she is still alive and despite the loss of her eye, she has chosen to forgive, to let go and to move on. She found the strength to transform her tragedy into a triumph by serving others who are in abusive relationships.

A key quality of Purpose is that it generally feels "bigger than you." We wonder, "How could I possibly accomplish *this*?" And the answer is that we can because our Soul knows we can, and it is waiting for us to *know* it too. We are so much more than we can imagine and we were made for more. And this is one of the fundamental causes of our sense of "there must be something more", because when we are aware, *we bring this to life through our life choices.* Because Sally accepted her Purpose in life instead of choosing to be a Victim, she was able to live her Destiny. She chose a higher level of consciousness and made the choice to forgive, and now her work as an advocate for healthy relationships changes the lives of thousands of people. That is how this works—what we experience in life prepares us for our True Purpose.

Be a Loving Warrior on a Mission

Living a life of Purpose is not for the faint of heart, and it definitely requires courage. However, you can reduce your fear by focusing on your vision instead of the details around how to make that vision reality. Your job is to know your *why*. The Universe will handle the *how*. Keep in mind that when we know the *why*, most of us can bear any *how*.

We must remember that the *why* is not "why me?" but rather "why not me?" If it happened, it served a Purpose and there is something there for you to know and grow from. Understanding why certain things occur for us during our journey (divorce, bankruptcy, heartbreak, health challenge, etc.), gives us the opportunity to view the situation from another perspective and empowers us to find a way to make something positive out of it and even strengthen our resolve and commitment to step more fully into who we are meant to be.

No matter how challenging your life has been so far, please know that there is a reason for it. What happens to you, and because of you, during your journey, is precisely designed for your Soul's evolution. Life is full of joy and pain, success and failure, and challenges are part of the game. It is the way of the hero, to embrace these challenges and consciously create a life well-lived. Even the suffering you have endured is unique and affects you uniquely. Become the kind of person who accepts what life has to offer and uses it for fertilizer to grow into someone magnificent.

Victor Frankl, who was fated to die in a WWII Nazi concentration camp, discovered that the number one reason people died in those camps was because prisoners gave up hope. Every day, he helplessly witnessed friends being escorted to the death chambers, and yet he trumped fate by deciding his own Destiny. Frankl realized that his internal perception could not be taken away by anyone or any thing outside of himself. He knew that *they* could not affect *his* internal mindset. Hope lived in his heart despite the fact that he was surrounded by such horrific circumstances.

Frankl went on to say, *"Everyone has his own specific vocation or mission in life to carry out a concrete assignment which demands fulfillment. Therein he cannot be replaced, nor can his life be repeated. Thus, everyone's task is as unique as his specific opportunity to implement it."* This wisdom tells us that our most important job is to find our "real work" and do it with all our heart. Frankl's *will to find meaning* kept him alive. Holding on to hope gave him a personal sense of empowerment that allowed him to make it through. Eventually he was released and went on to give us the gift of Logo therapy, which helps people find the meaning in their lives. His is a prime example of how our unique Destiny gives meaning to our existence and has a bearing on our creative work.

There will always be a healthy tension between what one is and what one can be because life is meant to challenge us to claim our Destiny – that which we 'can be'. Destiny is a moment by moment choice-making, ever-changing, dance. Stories such as Victor Frankl's and Sally's prove that anything can be overcome and that whatever adversity that you have experienced holds a seed of possibility. And when you choose a higher consciousness and live with love in your heart, you can transform anything into something magical and healing for yourself and others.

It bears repeating that all of your experiences are uniquely designed to awaken you to your truth, Purpose, and gifts. To find the meaning of your life, filter it through the highest consciousness you can as often as you can, because this will expand your ability to access infinite wisdom. In general, we can view life through our limited-self, our ego, or our higher self, our Soul.

Removing the Mask

When you walk through the world in *Victim, Victor,* or even *Vehicle* consciousness, you are wearing a mask, acting out a role, and even putting on an act. Don't make yourself wrong for this. We have all been doing for a very long time, out of a sense of survival. Because we are moving out of mere surviving into thriving, it's time to remove the mask.

Psychologist Carl Jung calls this our *persona*. In fact, the original term *persona* is a Latin origin and denotes a mask worn by an actor. Jung says that these are psychological skills we use to adapt to the outer world to help us see ourselves as acceptable and loveable. Sadly, we waste precious life force energy worrying about what other people think about us, when the truth is they are not really thinking about us much at all, *they are thinking about themselves.* What a funny and superficial way of interacting.

Wearing a mask or pretending to be something you are not only keeps you from becoming your True Self. Most importantly, we need to recognize and confront our underlying issues if we are to transcend the social masks that we hide behind. However it is when we become vulnerable and remove the masks that we can form meaningful bonds with others.

As we grow into wholeness, we can integrate all of our qualities, realizing that both the positive and the negative, the light and the dark are merely parts of who we are. We realize that we are acceptable and loveable just as we are, and only then can we learn to live on Purpose rather than by default in our familial and professional relationships.

Psychologists predict that 90% or more of human behavior comes from our subconscious mind, which runs like a broken tape recorder, playing the same thing over and over. When the subconscious controls our real life, something will happen in the present moment and an automatic switch is flipped in your memory bank reminding you of something from your past, and without thinking, you react based on this memory. Too often the reaction is negative, inappropriate, or not in your best interest. You see, we have all been conditioned by the limitations and expectations others have imposed upon us, what we saw our role models do, and from our collection of personal experiences.

By default, we "act out" what is in our subconscious programming. It is quite common to be unknowingly living out your parent's or even societal programming, rather than your own. For example, maybe you grew up with an emotionally unavailable father and you have become the same kind of person with your own children. You simply don't know what you don't know and therefore you continue to act almost like a computer that has been programmed by other people who also don't know.

The "mechanical mind" is programmed by the subconscious from past mental and emotional thoughts and feelings. And just like a tape that is played over and over again, your brain will keep running the same information in the same way, even when you receive new information, *until* you consciously choose to raise your consciousness.

Getting Your Ego on Board

Instead of being in harmony with all aspects of ourselves, we generally have an inner conflict going on between our ego and our Soul. For instance, we may say that want to know our Purpose and yet we still find ourselves pulled back into a default reality, full of dead-end jobs, unfulfilling relationships, stress and struggle. That's because even though at the Soul level all we truly desire is peace and happiness, our subconscious tape-player is enabling our ego (that loves to watch and listen to the same tapes over and over again) to rule our decisions by default – we're simply not paying enough attention to see that we're acting and reacting by rote.

A great majority of the population live their entire lifetimes with little or no awareness of their true greatness or potential. Why? Because we tend to listen to the loud and persistent voice of the ego instead of the small inner voice of the Soul. As a result, the ego blocks the discovery process and we miss the signposts and synchronicities that would lead to the life, relationship, or business of our dreams.

The ego *loves to search* but never find, mostly because it is afraid and needs a convenient excuse for not accepting the responsibility that comes with Greatness. Greatness would require the ego to expand and embrace changes that do not allow the constancy of the repeat tapes that are currently playing in your subconscious. It would require pressing the 'stop' button on the tape, and even creating entirely new tapes. This is far outside of the desired 'sameness' that the ego loves to live in.

It really does take *all of you* to access your potential and to succeed on Purpose, so let's look at how to get on board with your new life. The ego is like a first mate who is supposed to take orders from the captain, your Soul. If your ego is the one steering your ship, you will get taken off course again and again. Just like a ship that is seeking its perfect harbor, you need your Soul to guide you. And just as a ship experiences both easy sailing and stormy seas, you will have days when it is challenging to stay afloat.

Staying on course is important, though, as Charles Garfield once said: *"On course does not mean perfect. On course means that even when things don't go perfectly, you are still going in the right direction."* In fact, even when a ship is "on-course" it navigates the conditions through a constant state of zig-zagging and course corrections.

Limited Levels of Consciousness

The first three levels of consciousness, Victim, Victor and Vehicle, are vulnerable to different influences of the limited-self, specifically being *unaware, needy* or *seeking.*

The *Victim level* is all about you, and indicates you have not developed the psychological capacity to think beyond *your immediate survival needs.* You may be unaware that you have a higher Purpose.

The *Victor* level is so focused on learning and getting ahead that it has little time to care for anyone else. You are busy accumulating knowledge and things in order to support a *need for importance.*

Even though the *Vehicle* level is more integrated, the ego can still be at play. Especially when you think it is YOU writing the book, singing the song, or painting the picture. Here you are *seeking* status or recognition.

It is through the Divine, perhaps through what you may experience as intuition and inspiration, that the most beautiful things are created. When you live and vibrate *Vessel* consciousness, you simply allow your gifts or creations to emerge, with little thought for recognition, payment, or other worldly accolades. Not many people have reached that level of consciousness, although that is humanity's greatest Destiny—to employ our best selves to do the work of the Divine. The simple fact that you are reading this material means that you are *willing* and that is all that is required.

In an attempt to stay protected, our limited-self will create beliefs that we are "confused" and "don't know who we are." "After all," the limited-self says, "who are we to be bright, brilliant, powerful human beings who are here to change the world for the better?" Acting confused or playing dumb simply blocks your power. Choose instead to bravely and boldly shine the light that you are because the new world needs ***bright lights*** who are open-hearted, strong-minded, and committed to being a force for positive change.

Developing a Healthy Ego

You may find it challenging to shift from a state of being unaware to becoming aware, as your ego can be a very powerful trickster, sabotaging your best efforts. For instance you may sabotage your progress by placing yourself in environments that are not good for you. If your friends or spouse bring you down, or are negative, you will find it harder to break out of old habits and social circles. As you reach higher levels of consciousness you will more carefully select the people with whom you choose to associate, and begin to spend time with those who uplift you. Likewise, you can become stuck working in a position that doesn't value, validate, or encourage your true gifts and natural talents.

Generally speaking, most of us fall into a trap of common ways of being, living a mediocre life with little growth or vitality. Let me assure you, there is nothing wrong with letting go of people and situations that you have outgrown. Be careful not to fall prey to self-judgments, the expectations of others, or socially induced ideas about moving on. Most people stay in unhealthy situations far longer than necessary because they have not developed the spiritual skill of letting go. This is where a healthy ego is required, to help you erect appropriate boundaries between what is right for you and what is not.

This includes YOU—do not try to make the ego wrong or kill it off.... it won't work anyway. Instead of trying to get rid of the ego, integrate the ego and love it. Ego-integration means you accept this part of yourself and are able to find a healthy balance, where it follows the lead of your Soul.

Until the ego is integrated, you may fall into "default mode." A *mode is* a habituated way of being that occurs without conscious thought. The most common default *personal strategy* is people-pleasing and emotional manipulation. The most common default *professional strategy* is chasing money and opportunity. If you ever find yourself enacting these strategies, simply pause and choose differently.

Many successful people have well-developed egos, the difference is that they do not let their ego control them. People who are over-inflated and think that "it's all about me" are irritating at best. On the reverse side, the equally unappealing "I'm nobody" and "I am not worthy" kind of people lack the required level of moxie to be effective in the world. Many people who are here to make the biggest difference too often suffer from an under-developed ego, and in fact seem much more afraid of their brilliance and light than of anything else.

It makes sense—from the moment we were born, we were programmed to believe that our source of power is outside of us and that we were separated and unworthy of receiving it. On some level you fear being all of who you are. My coaching practice is called *Bright Light Coaching* because for a long time I resisted and denied my own brilliance, which is precisely why I am so great at helping others move past their resistance so they can shine their light.

Denial of our greatness and Divinity is the greatest sin (error) that humans have inherited. In The Gospel of Thomas, Jesus said: *"If you bring forth what is within you, what you bring forth will save you. If you do not bring forth what is within you, what you do not bring forth will destroy you."* I believe he was speaking about our Divinity and that by recognizing and choosing to own it, is what is meant by *living in the Kingdom.*

Sit with the idea that you are an aspect of the Divine incarnated, and consider that you have much more to offer than you previously realized or were willing to own up to. Coming to that realization, and surrendering the controls to your higher self, you will find that life becomes much more interesting indeed!

Once you reach *Vessel* level consciousness, *"I am my Purpose,"* you simply are who you were born to be. In the Allowance stage, you flow with the river of your consciously chosen reality. In the meantime, the more you can let your limited-self relax and get out of the way, the more your Soul can lead you exactly where you are meant to go with perfect timing. You really can work in harmony with this part of you.

We will be talking more about resistance, resignation, and the saboteur in the next section. For now, just let your ego know that you are secure. Remind yourself that living your life on Purpose will give you all of the success, recognition, and abundance that *all of you* desires.

Everyday Enlightenment

A healthy ego empowers us to know who we are and what we stand for, which is especially important if we are going to be standing out from the crowd.

Journal Entry 5: 44 Essential Things About Me

Since your ego loves to talk about "me," here is your chance to talk yourself up! Write:

- *11 Things I love about my life*
- *11 Things that are uniquely me*
- *11 things I like to talk about or teach*
- *11 things I would change in the world*

Self-Coaching Exercise:
Identifying Your Soul Essence

There are eight soul essences reflective of spiritual gifts that can each be represented by a color of the rainbow. Read through these and discover which color you resonate most with.

Red: *You may be the leader*. The person that feels passionate about having a big vision, taking charge, and leading others.

Orange: *You may be the promoter*. The person that feels passionate about getting the word out to others.

Yellow: *You may be the thinker*. The person who has the capacity to see the big picture, and intuit what is most important to pay attention to.

Green: *You may be the fixer*. The person other people can count on to figure things out when something requires adjustment.

Blue: *You may be the teacher*. The person who everyone comes to for guidance about how to do something.

Indigo: *You may be the healer*. The person that feels passionate about healing and nurturing others to be their best selves.

Violet: *You may be the connector*. The person that feels passionate about connecting souls with each other because of a deep feeling that certain folks are meant to meet.

White: *You may be the supporter*. The person that feels passionate about being supportive to others and organizations.

Of course, you may have a favorite color of your own and can come up with a quality that matches who you think you are. My favorite color is bright pink and I see that as a mixture of red, blue, and purple. This reflects my spiritual gifts of being a visionary leader, teacher/guide, and healer. Which color are you?

Stage Three: Acceptance

"God has given us our marching orders. Our purpose here on earth is to find those orders and carry them out. Those orders acknowledge our spiritual gifts." —Soren Kierkegaard

Stage Three: Acceptance

Acceptance is the third stage of the *Destiny Discovery Process* where you accept many new ideas about who you really are as well as your personal and professional Purposes. There are two detours you need to watch out for in this stage:

~ believing what society tells you is normal, or what you should do, instead of what you know is true for you, and

~ listening to your saboteur's (ego's) critical voices instead of listening to the voice of your Soul.

When you are in acceptance, you begin to embrace the idea that your life has meaning and Purpose and that it is your job to be and do whatever is called for. You come to a place of agreement with yourself about discovering how to best bring forth what is within you. Once you truly accept your path, you will free up a lot of anxious and depressed energy that was previously bottled up from being disconnected from your inner brilliance.

The reason why many people seem to stall at this stage is because there is more than one thing to come to terms with. Since you may have lived your life mostly in resistance and resignation, acceptance may elude you for a while. Remember that we are often more afraid of our light and greatness than anything else.

With acceptance there is nothing you have to do or even say to anyone else. Here, you are focused on getting into alignment with your own heart, and accepting the authentic you (warts and all) unconditionally. The next stage, Articulation, is where you will finally be able to communicate your Purpose. The biggest key to acceptance is integrating what you became aware of in the Awareness (stage 2), that you are more than your body, personality, and belief systems; that, in fact, you are an unlimited Soul, full of infinite potential, light and love.

This is the stage many of my clients find themselves stuck in. Through energetic alignment processes, I help them to heal the resistance and resignation that their inner saboteur creates to keep them in the status quo. This chapter may bring up some of your own "mental monsters" but stick with me, and you will get where you are meant to go.

Here are five things to accept:

1. The Past: Accept everything that has occurred. Embrace what has happened to you, including what worked well and what felt disastrous, for it all brought you to this point. Accept that on some level you needed to experience what has been to become what you are.

2. Yourself: Accept that you are worthy and deserving of being truly loved and succeeding beyond your wildest dreams. Remember that you may not have been told how worthy and deserving you are and so you may not feel "good enough" to live a truly great life. Now is the time to stop denying your brilliance and to shine your light.

3. Possibility: Accept that you have a life Purpose that is bigger than you. Everybody's Purpose could be summed up as "being authentically happy and expressing my true self." Accept that this is your birthright and realize that when you choose to be authentically happy, miracles happen.

4. Unique Blessing: Accept that your Divine gifts help others in the world. You do not have to know how you will share your unique blessing yet, or even have the words to articulate it. You are simply getting used to the idea of being a healer, teacher, leader, etc. Your blessing is often bigger than your limited-self could imagine, so be open to the expansion of how to best express the essence of who you are.

5. Your Divinity: As a *vessel* for the Divine, you possess Divine attributes such as, love, kindness, goodness, gentleness, humor, faithfulness, love, joy, peace, strength, and wisdom. The accumulation of "everyday enlightenment experiences" has given you the opportunity to cultivate at least one of these Divine attributes. Accept that this is your very precious gift to give.

Since this is quite a bit to digest, let's take a moment to do an energetic alignment exercise before we go on.

Acceptance: an Energetic Alignment Exercise

We spend a lot of energy "searching for ourselves" in various places, adventures and experiences, and more specifically, where we are *not*. This exercise will help you to recover some of that lost energy by accepting what has been, what is, and what will be. Start by choosing to feel what it is like to "accept" where you are, right here, right now. Now think about your past and breathe acceptance into all that has happened. Allow yourself to really be with this deep feeling of acceptance, knowing you are exactly where you are meant to be. Accept yourself, all of yourself. Give yourself a moment to fully BE with how *Acceptance* feels. Next, open yourself up to accepting a new possibility for your life. Be with this for a moment and imagine where you are, what you are doing, who you are with. Move to seeing your Soul Essence or the unique blessing that you are and accept this. See yourself being a contribution to other people's lives just by being you. Finally, accept your Divinity, and that you are made to shine your unique love and light. Once you accept something with your whole heart, you create a neutral space which will then generate positive power and energy. At this point, you begin to open yourself up to receive a new possibility for your life.

If you bump up against resistance, resignation or fear as you read through this chapter or even the book, simply return to this exercise.

Destiny Practice:
I AM One with the Divine living in the body as ______(your name).
I have the power to choose the Destiny I want to be a part of.

Accepting Your Divine Assignment

As you own what makes you truly great, it is much easier to accept your higher Purpose. Like the diamond analogy I used earlier, many of us spend a lifetime searching for our Purpose outside of ourselves in some role or position. The 13th Century poet, Rumi warns us, *"You wander from room to room hunting for the diamond necklace that is already around your neck."* We look everywhere but within until we accept that *we are* what we are seeking. And remember that no matter where you find yourself, in a default or pseudo or personality purpose, through acceptance you can choose to be happy no matter what your circumstance.

And with acceptance, it is much easier to begin again when your Soul is calling for it.

There is a phrase "everyone is called but few are chosen" that I would like to discuss. To me, this means that only some of us will use our free will to do the inner work necessary to fulfill our Divine Destiny. Only a few will 'accept their assignment.' Keep in mind this does not make us special, at least not in an ego sense. However, it does mean that we answered the call of our Soul, and that is special, it can even been considered *greatness embodied.* A life of Destiny is a rare commodity, much like a rare jewel, and is bestowed upon those who walk through the fires of their own personal transformation and live their Purpose.

After we accept our mission, as it were, is when the real training begins. We then become *qualified* by enduring the many tests that may come our way designed to strengthen our character and expand our capacity to love.

The *Acceptance* stage is by no means a straight shot; rather, it can be likened to a labyrinth, with twists and turns and starts and stops, while you are constantly striving to reach the center. To walk the *Destiny Discovery* path is to be aware, awake, and consciously learning our Soul's lessons so that we can evolve; it is definitely one of the most daunting decisions we could ever make during our lifetime. Many people remain at the lower levels without truly accessing their Soul's power by choosing the mastery level of life. Too many people get complacent and stop short of their Destiny—and with the changes we are seeing in the world, we need every single Destiny-based human we can get!

Obviously there is a big difference between how life shows up from level one (our default purpose), level two (our pseudo purpose), level three (our personality purpose) and level four, our Soul Purpose and Destiny.

Jeanne was doing a wonderful job as the announcement leader for her church. She was so close to her true calling, even speaking and inspiring others from behind the podium. She was bright, loving and seemed to really enjoy what she was doing. Yet inside, she was called to be more influential, to do more with her gifts. She wanted to be a Minister. She made the decision to take the leap of faith, and started taking classes. Within two years of intensive training, she achieved her goal. Today, she is behind the very same podium as the new leader of that same church, but now shining her *brightest light,* because she followed her Purpose to where it wanted to take her. She allowed herself to give up being successful, and comfortable, as her Personality Purpose (level three) to live her Destiny. You can choose to play at a higher level by living your Destiny too. When you step forward in faith and allow your light to shine, you become an inspiration for others to do the same.

Once you are well on the path, you will find that you flow with life's changes, challenges, and obstacles with more ease and grace. Your direction will seem clearer and easier because your operating system has been upgraded to one of personal faith (**F**inding **A**nswers **I**n **T**he **H**eart). You now have a solid belief that all is right with the world, and an inner peace with your life's direction. You will no longer get stressed about what the future holds, you will be certain that your future will unfold as it is meant to and you will learn to stay in alignment with the frequency of Divine love by practicing energy alignment techniques.

Everyday Enlightenment

You were given a blueprint full of potential, and it is your great pleasure to follow it and create from that innate image something amazing in this reality!

Critical Voices

As you have a look within to discover your greatness, you may encounter a shadowy-looking character. It is not "real" per se, but can take on a life of its own, and it is known as a saboteur. According to Caroline Myss, author and medical intuitive, human beings have four survival archetypes (orphan, prostitute, child, and saboteur) that help us get our needs met. When in balance, they can serve us well, alerting us to dangerous liaisons or poor decisions. But more often than not, one or more of the critical voices in your head drowns out the *one voice* that knows where you are meant to go. We will focus on the saboteur and it's various voices so that you can recognize the difference between the voices in *your* head.

The Bully: "you can't"

This voice is dominating and will tell you that you are not good enough and that you *can't*. If you believe you have limits, you will never actualize your potential, and as Henry Ford said, *"whether you think you can or can't, you are right."*

How to handle: Drop *I can't* from your vocabulary and ask, *What is possible?* Claim what you want by saying *I Will, I Am.*
Affirm: *I can do anything I set my mind and heart to.*

The Boss: "you should/ought to/must"

This voice is authoritarian and tries to make you feel guilty. It can come from your own head or from others who advise you, in particular friends and family. You may feel anxiety when you encounter situations for which your *should's, must's,* and *ought to's* do not seem to apply. This leads to a constant inner battle with what "they" say you should do versus what your Soul is calling for you to do.

How to handle: Replace should, ought to, and must with *I choose or I choose not to.* Making a choice will be accompanied by a feeling of excitement, and initial fear, and increased personal freedom.
Affirm: *I choose to follow my internal guidance system.*

The Confused: "indecision/hem and haw"

This voice is insecure and may say things like "I don't know what to do or who I am." It aims to prevent you from owning your personal power by having you stay in limbo. Being confused is a good excuse for not taking action.

How to handle: Become aware of your true desires and express them clearly with confidence, knowing that you are deserving and worthy of receiving what you ask for.
Affirm: *I trust myself to make wise choices.*

The Dark: "I fear the unknown," "I don't like change"
This voice is ominous and scary, and will keep you in the dark, unable to see ahead so you can move forward. You will not venture out of your comfort zone to learn or expand, which keeps you stuck.

How to handle: When you get scared, rant for 10 minutes about what you are afraid of, get it all out. And then ask yourself, *if this happens, what does that mean?* Keep asking and '*what does that mean*' until you come to your underlying fear. Then focus on what is real by grounding yourself. Hold your hand on your heart and stomach and say: "I trust myself to handle anything that comes my way. I step forward confidently."
Affirm: *I courageously follow my path of Purpose, no matter where it leads. I follow Spirit without hesitation.*

Do not think you are the only one with voices in your head. The famous artist, Vincent Van Gogh said, *"If you hear a voice inside your head telling you are not a painter then paint and that voice will be silent."* Van Gogh bypassed that voice by painting and we receive the benefit of him winning the battle over his saboteur. You can do the same.

Journal Entry 6: Getting Unstuck

Use these questions whenever you are feeling stuck in life.
What is the most loving thing I could do right now?
What would love do?
Where can I be more loving in my relationships, in my work, for myself?

Healing Your Inner Saboteur

Success in life comes much easier when you develop the ability to override the limiting and sabotaging voices inside in favor of listening to your Soul's guidance. So what is an *inner saboteur*? The saboteur is the part of you that pulls you off track with self-defeating behaviors that keep you stuck. It loves the status quo and goes into resistance when positive change comes around. The saboteur seems real and has its own voice and demeanor, but is nothing more than a "thought energy." It exists because you invented it at some point during your life to stay safe and to play small.

The main goal is to thwart your efforts, to make you think negatively and even manifest external excuses like a sore throat, flat tire, headache, etc. Keep in mind that this kind of behavior usually occurs just when you begin to make forward progress.

The saboteur feeds off of resignation and resistance and is a lackey of the ego. It stands at alert, hyper-vigilant, guarding the door that leads to your Destiny. By the way, it is only doing the job that your ego told it to do, which is to limit how much joy, abundance, love, and money you get to have in life. Since you created it, you can re-create it. You might ask yourself, "What percentage of my life is the saboteur running?" If it is more than 5% then adjustments can and should be made.

To *sabotage* means to take deliberate action aimed at weakening an enemy, oppressor or employer through subversion, obstruction, or destruction. When you "self-sabotage," what this means is that you are in direct conflict with yourself and your desires. You may want to get on your true path one moment, then the next moment you are not so sure or you may even become frozen with fear. *You move towards it, and then run away from it.* It's like having your foot on the gas and the brake at the same time and staying stuck. Sound familiar? This behavior can be obvious or devastatingly subtle, but when it is you who is perpetrating it against yourself, it is often hard to recognize.

All you know is that your life, relationship, or career is just not working. You may have tried to fight or resist this voice, but resistance is quite futile.

Just like a small child or animal needs love and affection, so does this part of you. The saboteur wants to be useful to you and it has a genuine need to be heard, so when you don't give it the attention it needs and demands, it will act out. It may even manifest in self-destructive behavior or make you ill.

One of my clients, John, is a powerful business man. He noticed an obvious sign when his saboteur would act up. Anytime he decided to go to the next level in his business, he would experience an allergic reaction, with runny nose, sneezing—the whole stuffy head syndrome. Through our work together, he began making "Grumpy" (that was his saboteur's name) a friend. He gave Grumpy a new role and learned how to "sooth his saboteur." Now, whenever he decides to play a bigger game, he has all of himself working cooperatively and 'voila' forward progress is made.

If you are wondering if you have one, just ask,
"Do I have a saboteur inside?" And allow yourself to 'hear' the answer.

You have one too, eh? Welcome to being human. If you truly desire to live a life of Destiny, the best thing to do is seek out and receive emotional support. Just realize that when you hire a coach or enroll in a transformational program, this part of you may get nervous because it feels that things are changing, and probably changing quickly. It also does not like taking into account another's point of view, especially someone who is an "authority". The saboteur loves to think it is always right even though most of the time it is way off base. You have to love how committed it is to its own way of thinking—limited though it may be!

Recall how powerful you can be when you have both your limited and higher self working together harmoniously? Work at befriending your saboteur so that it is on board with your Purpose-centered life. I learned about the saboteur early on in my coaching career and made it a point to have a *heal your inner saboteur process* where my clients learn to befriend the saboteur by accepting, loving, and promoting it to a position it is better suited for. Because it is so good at being "on guard," it often likes the Discernment Department. What we do is energetically move the saboteur into their heart and have it take up residence there, so that it begins filtering stimuli through wisdom and love. By integrating this part of the client's psyche for something useful, the work of personal transformation goes much easier and results come more quickly too.

Resistance to change is the number one reason your path is blocked, as it shuts off your Divine connection. Resistance is what stands between you and having what you want. It often surfaces when we get close to breaking through old programs and ways of being, showing up in every conceivable way—from limited thinking, to actually refusing to do what you know you need to do, to suddenly feeling sick, etc. As you can imagine, resistance is a common ploy of the saboteur. When you are in resistance, see it as a signpost that you are headed in the right direction, embrace feeling uncomfortable and keep walking in faith.

Resignation will block you from even trying to make changes. Resignation looks and feels very heavy; like you are being weighed down or held back. Resignation is destructive to your Soul because it takes positive energy and new possibilities and squelches them before they ever have a chance to take root, thus you feel somewhat suffocated and unexpressed. When resignation threatens to take away your possibility thinking, call upon your mentor or friend, so they can talk you through the "why even try" story you may be buying into.

Life becomes easier and more fulfilling when you honor yourself by following the energy of what feels good and true for you. Focus on cultivating a positive mindset, asking powerful questions and practicing excellent self-care. In most cases, emotional healing and energetic balancing can help clear your inner channel so you can become the *Vessel* for consciousness that you were born to be. Here are some additional ways to soothe your inner saboteur.

Self-Coaching Exercise:
Ways to Soothe the Saboteur

- Learn to ask empowering questions: What acceptance can I be here? What greatness can I be? Can I let this go? What else is possible? What do I want or need right now? What will empower me to feel good? What lesson am I learning?

- Befriend your saboteur. Get to know it by journaling or dialoguing with it. You can even give it a name. Listen with non-attachment, and if the voice is especially belligerent, say “thank you for sharing” and move on.

- Be supported in your personal growth process. Mentoring helps you to heal the saboteur, and it also empowers you to identify your blind spots so you can clearly see the best route to take towards your success.

Facing Fears

A common definition for fear in the self-help field is *"False Evidence Appearing Real."* This acronym illustrates how human beings often confuse what is good for us as something to fear. Since greatness often lies in the "unknown zone" and invites change, we hold ourselves back.

Many times, we act as if our life is really in danger, when it is simply our Soul asking us to grow. Obviously, fear had its place in the caveman days when we needed to know if there was a Saber Tooth Tiger on the prowl. And, of course, if there is a threat to our safety—that kind of fear makes sense. Real fear keeps you safe, but false fear keeps you stuck. Learning to know the difference will empower you to break free from old patterns and write a successful script for the life of your dreams.

The most common fear is *fear of change*, because it upsets our way of doing things. As creatures of habit, we like things to remain the same, and stepping into our Purpose may mean we have to grow beyond our immature and selfish ways into someone mature and generous.

Another fear I have seen in regards to living on Purpose is that you may have *missed the boat* that you thought you were supposed to be on. Keep in mind that whatever you did before was your 'training ground' for your Purpose, so you are exactly where you are supposed to be. You can also reject the idea that "it's too late for me to be what I was supposed to be." Most people do not come into their True Purpose until their 30's, 40's, 50's, or even beyond, as it takes a lot of seasoning from life experiences to have the capacity and maturity to be who you were born to be.

Two other fears that block Destiny are *fear of our greatness and the fear of intimacy*, which are the very experiences that we most deeply crave. Without close, loving relationships and success in our creative endeavors, we feel like something important is missing from life. Have you noticed that just when we get close to having what we want, like a great relationship or new career, something strange happens—old ideas and memories of disappointment start projecting from our past right into our future, thus messing with our good intentions?

These images, feelings, and scenarios are part of the *story* that we keep telling ourselves, and prevent us from living our Destiny. Comfort zones give us a false sense of security, and we even try to convince ourselves that we are "just fine" with the status quo. The fact is, we are uncomfortable, and need to change.

When it comes to Purpose, what stops many from answering the call of the Soul is *fear of not having enough money, stability, security,* etc. In regards to money and abundance, we have to overcome our collective lack consciousness and see the abundance of the very world we live in. To see the leaves on a tree, flowers in the field, grains of sand on the beach, fish in the sea, as evidence that there is more than enough for all to enjoy.

As author Alan Cohen says, *"The economy is an expression of the consciousness of those who create it, all of us. We vitalize the economy with expansive thinking and action, and we deaden it with fear and contraction. You have power over the economy, especially your own, by consciously choosing the thoughts you think, the attitudes you hold, and the actions that proceed from them."* Since we collectively create our reality, it is up to as many of us as possible to cultivate the ability to hold the higher vision, especially when times are tough.

Money comes to people who know how to use their skills and talents, and there will always be new creations out of chaos. Plato said it best *"Necessity is the mother of invention."* In fact, it is when the world is in need of something that commerce and purpose can come together to create something new and different, consider modern examples like cell phones and the internet.

Napolean Hill, who studied the most successful people of his time, such as Thomas Edison and John D. Rockefeller, wrote the classic book *Think and Grow Rich,* where he discusses a link between having a *Definite Purpose* and the ability to make a lot of money and succeed in life. For the first time in human history, we have the unique opportunity to take charge of our personal economy and be responsible for our financial future by earning a living while making a positive difference.

Fear grips us hardest when we step into *unknown territory*—we simply don't know what to expect or if we can handle it. When you are fearful, realize it's probably due to the uncertainty you are feeling about the future, which can be easily faced with faith in yourself and by relying on others. Ironically, *fear of success* often trumps fear of failure. We are most frightened of our brilliance and power; and so we play small, settling for less than our heart's true desires. After all, we are familiar with things *not working* out, so when things actually get really good, a strange feeling overtakes us.

When you are experiencing change and growth, just remember, you come from Greatness and were made from Greatness, so, it follows that *Greatness is what you really are.* As you can guess, fear cuts off a lot of valuable energy that could be used to create what you really want. So when fears come bubbling up, face them knowing it is okay to feel uncertain and embrace your True Self. The presence of fear is a sign that your limited self is relying on your own strength and will power and you have gotten out of alignment with your greatness.

Have you noticed that once you do the thing you fear or even come to an understanding of it, the fear dissipates as if it were nothing but a cloud in the sky? From this moment on, notice the fear, but don't give it power; simply focus on what you want and then *take action*. You will soon forget what all the drama was about. Remember that with the right education and support you can expand your capacity to handle any amount of success that may come your way.

When you shine the bright light of awareness on your fears, all that is left is clarity. Clarity is power. And when you are 'empowered,' nothing can stop you. Now that you have befriended your saboteur and faced your fear, it's time to articulate and take the right actions which will lead you to the Destiny you have dreamed of, and yes, you can get used to having things work in your favor.

Journal Entry 7: Release Fear

Why do I feel resistance or resignation?
What am I afraid of?
What is the worst that could happen?
What is the best that could happen?
What is the probable outcome?
What action can I take now to move me forward at least one step?

Self-Coaching Exercise:
Instant Energetic Alignment
Sit up straight, and imagine a golden light being poured into your crown chakra (which is located at the top of your head) melting away any resistance, doubts or fears. Breathe in love. Place your hand over your heart and sacral (belly) chakras and say *I trust myself and the Universe to protect and provide for me.*

Affirm:
I love me.
I am doing everything right.
I choose powerfully.
I celebrate my choices.
I choose the Destiny I want to be a part of!
I advance. I revise. I expand.

Stage Four: Articulation

"When you are inspired by some great purpose, some extraordinary project, all your thoughts break their bonds. Your mind transcends limitations, your consciousness expands in every direction, and you find yourself in a new, great, and wonderful world. Dormant forces, faculties and talents become alive, and you discover yourself to be a greater person by far than you ever dreamed yourself to be."
—Patanjali

Stage Four: Articulation

Articulation is the fourth stage in the *Destiny Discovery Process* where you put your personal and professional Purposes into words. There are two detours to watch out for in this stage:

~ becoming entangled in unhealthy relationships, and

~ falling into a false Purpose trap in your career.

It's very easy to get caught in the *Deadly D* of denial here. Once you have committed to a new path and Purpose, the ego wants to be right and will trick you into believing that what you have is "real," even though it may be something that's just a substitute for the real thing. When you reach this stage you have integrated a lot of your truth and are now clear enough to communicate to others what you are truly up to in the world.

Articulation is the process of creation and a precursor to action. It gives you the structure upon which to be more intentional with your way of being. Intentionality is a hallmark of success and the more clearly you can state your declaration, the more power is behind it. The process of writing down your Purposes and reflecting on them will accelerate bringing them into reality.

Affirming through writing and speaking about your Purpose helps to make it real, and allows you to move beyond the ego-mind of fear, rationalizing, settling or talking yourself out of it. When you truly own your Purpose and it resonates with every cell in your body, it will become very easy to see when others are trying to dissuade you out of jealousy or fear—you will be supremely confident in your knowing and you will own your Purpose without hesitation.

Let's look at the power of choosing your language and words carefully. Words have power because they carry the force of your intention out into the world, they are literally "casting a spell." What you *say* is often what you *see*. Whenever you speak or write what you intend there is more power and potency if you do it from a feeling of alignment.

This is not new idea; even ancient Egyptians believed that words were magic. They believed that if you wrote it, it would surely happen. In this stage, you are going to state your *Destiny Declarations* so that you have clearly set intentions for what you want to create in your relationships and chosen vocation.

Destiny Practice:
How great can I create myself today? Write out your intention: Today I am filled with enthusiasm and satisfaction for my work and life.

Journal Entry 8: Life Vision

Begin by writing a life vision, which is the overall blueprint for your life. Write out in detail how you would like your life to be in regards to health, wealth, work, relationships, and fun. Keep in mind the energetic Universe that we live in. Know that your thoughts, words, and actions create either your default reality or your Destiny.

Start with a blessing: I open myself to the creative source of all life. Spirit is. I am. We are. I am at one with the wholeness, intelligence, grace, power, and truth of life itself. I welcome inspiration and insight to flow through me in this new vision for my life.

When you complete your visioning process:

You might say, "Thank you for the Divine inspiration and vision that is revealing itself to me. I bless myself and all of creation."

Personal Purpose
Your Personal Purpose relates to your relationships. It's your way of being nurturing with yourself, others, and the Universe. We need to be all of who we are to enjoy the relationships and experiences that bring us joy.

You can either live out your *false purpose* or your *true purpose* in your relations with others. You may fall into *false purpose* when you are on auto-pilot and are not consciously aware of how you are reacting to what life throws at you. You may say, "Not this again," and feel a sense of discontentment. Unless you make conscious the decisions and actions that are running you, you will live out a *false* purpose; one that does not reflect who you really are, and who you were born to be. You'll fail to wake up from the trance you are in, to see beyond your physical self, and recognize your spiritual self.

Our default personal purpose is how we *gain* attention from others and is created from ego.
Our true personal purpose is how we *show* attention to others and flows from the soul.

You've probably heard the Shakespearian quote, *"All the world is a stage."* It is quite true that we unconsciously play out our roles in life; much like actors in a play. We also create and write scenes with the underlying motivation to gain attention from our audience in order to feel good about ourselves. Until we are awakened, much of what we do is designed to "look good" to ourselves and others.

So, in the story of your life, you are often *unconsciously* creating, directing, and acting out the scenes. Fear of rejection keeps you in your *ego role* which is limited and fear-based. Learning to accept *what is,* as well as *what is not,* empowers you to step into your *Soul role*; which is expansive and love-based.

Common stories of the ego/limited-self:

"I am not good enough."
"I am unworthy."
"Life is disappointing."
"I have to be in control."
"Life is hard."
"Nobody loves me."
"The world is not safe."
"I have to please people in order to be liked or accepted."

Our *default* way of being develops quite early in childhood, until about seven years of age, and is primarily based on experiences that were negative or didn't feel good. Our early decisions may have been based in fear and the fundamental need to have our basic needs met. Let's take a moment to consider the word *default*: "to fail to do what is required," "an absence or lack of." Think also of a computer's default programs; unless we change the programs we are using or upgrade them, they will continue to run exactly the same way continuously.

We can unknowingly become *hung up* on past ideas. Our *hang-ups* are typically revealed when something is done or said to us and we have an extreme reaction to it (based on programming from the past). Often, we aren't even aware of why we feel the way we do. These behaviors come from many different experiences you had as a child, including unmet expectations.

As a result, when you react now you may throw a temper tantrum, gobble up center stage in a group of people, over-give, get defensive, act like a spoiled brat, withdraw, or become invisible, etc. the same way you learned to do as a child to get what you wanted or needed.

Often you cannot see your behavior, but others do. As I have mentioned, we attempt to keep ourselves safe by forming *personas;* ways of being that help us survive in the world. These masks lead to *false purpose traps* that prevent us from living as our *True Self.*

Behavioral clues that you are relating from your default programming:

Regression: You regress to a more primitive level of personality and social development. You may become like a little child, whine or cry, or act like a teenager and rebel.

Overly Emotional: The more emotional (angry, frustrated, upset) you are, the less ability you have to adapt. You may "fly off the handle" or even throw things.

Projection: You blame your feelings on someone or something else. You may view the source of your feelings as being caused by something "out there" and not "in here".

Persistence: You hang on to the negative thought, image, or emotion; unable to think of anything else. You may make yourself miserable, sick, or stressed as a result.

Each of these reactions are a result of how you perceive your life has been until now. At any moment, you can invent a new possibility, and therefore a new reaction, for yourself. The more you are aware of how your default personal purpose is running your life, the easier it will be to self-correct and get back into harmony, love, and acceptance with yourself and others.

Seven Signs You Are Living Your True Personal Purpose

Your Personal Purpose inspires you to connect and relate to yourself, others, and the world.

1. You are unfiltered and do not hide your light.
2. You see the best in yourself and others.
3. You practice forgiveness and compassion.
4. You are forthright when speaking your Truth.
5. You live in the present moment.
6 You are grateful and happy for "no reason."
7. People enjoy being around you and you enjoy being with them.

Self-Coaching Exercise:
Uncover Your Default Program

Imagine your life as a movie:
What is the movie's theme or main story line?
What kind of movie is it — a tragedy, comedy, drama, or love story?
What is your victim story?
What challenges did you face?
What are some of the key lessons of your life?
How do you feel when you watch this movie?
What is your theme song?
How are the people in your life responding to you?
How are you responding to others?

Professional Purpose

The *Professional Purpose* relates to the kind of impact you want to have on the world in the form of your contribution. The famous artist, Vincent Van Gogh said, *"Your profession is not what brings home your paycheck.*

Your profession is what you were put on earth to do with such passion and intensity that it becomes a spiritual calling." It's not about what you think you should be doing, or even what you can do well; it's about what calls you.

What I have seen is that many people either ignore or can't hear the call because they are disconnected from their Soul. All they know is that something important is missing.

In today's modern world of work, people want more meaning from the work that they do. Traditionally, you got a job, hung on to it, and more than likely retired with it. In the 21st century world of work you are free to choose to do anything you would like. Options are endless and when you combine that with the fact that experts predict that you will change career fields (not just jobs) 7-10 times in your life, it is easy to get overwhelmed with too many choices. The trick here is to choose the right path that will lead you where you want to go without getting side-tracked or *off purpose.*

Many modern people have mistakenly limited their career decisions based on titles or roles. For instance: Johnnie gets the idea of becoming an accountant from his parents who believe that is steady work. But after he goes through college and is a practicing CPA, he finds that he is not feeling fulfilled at all. At this point, he cannot see any other possibilities for himself, and may even feel purposeless. He might wonder, "Who am I Now?" "What am I meant to be doing?" "Isn't it too late in the game to change careers?"

To keep this from happening to you, it is important to decide how you want to serve other people. Instead of limiting yourself to a specific role, like accountant, you may discover that your Purpose is *to perform work that helps people live wealthier lives.* This now provides several options, such as CPA, financial consultant, business executive or __________?

Being able to clearly articulate what your *Professional Purpose is* helps you to make successful career, and life, transitions; which is something that you will be doing throughout your lifetime. It is safe to say that when most people lose a job or an important position, they do not know what to do with themselves. This is because their identity is tied so closely to their job title. On the other hand, a person who has discovered his or her Purpose will attract new work that allows them to be, or at least further discover, who they are.

Our ego's false professional purpose is a "getting" mentality.
Our soul's true professional purpose is a "giving" mentality.

Are you still trying to figure out what you want to be when you grow up? The smarter question is: what gifts do I have that the world needs? Professional Purpose is more than just having a job or career. It is sharing your knowledge, skills, and unique abilities with the world in a way that is uniquely you. It's like having your own brand, doing it in your own special way; *you* are your own special sauce!

To choose wisely, create your work and career around your desired lifestyle. Choose work that allows you to apply your passions (things you love to do) and allows you to express yourself. Make sure that your chosen work is in alignment with your *internal motivators* and values — those things that are closest to your heart. Values are the things that are a priority for you. For example, perhaps you value personal expression and creativity, in that case it would be best to avoid working in highly structured or system-based roles.

External motivators are things like money, power, and control. They are all about looking good to yourself and others.

Internal motivators are things like a sense of pride, wanting to make a contribution, and personal satisfaction.

Why try to put your square peg in a round hole? And yet people often fall into positions that go against their core values and end up suffering stress-related health issues, such as burn-out, ulcers, migraines, etc. Whenever you have an internal conflict, or feel something is not right, then you can bet it is due to the fact that you are in a situation or relationship that does not support your value system. Learn to do things for the *sheer enjoyment* of it, and you are sure to have stumbled upon a way to fulfill your deepest calling.

Seven Signs You Are Living Your True Professional Purpose
Your Professional Purpose inspires you to create and contribute.

1. You feel called or compelled to do it, you simply can't avoid it.
2. You lose track of time when you are doing it.
3. You love to talk about it whenever you get the chance.
4. You want to teach others what you know.
5. You are excited to get out of bed in the morning.
6. You would do it even if you did not get paid.
7. You feel like there is something bigger coming through you.

Self-Coaching Exercise:
Choosing a Possible Path
You can come back to this exercise as often as needed when you feel off-path. Answer yes or no to the following:

Am I living my personal purpose? Yes ____ No ____
If no, this is because I do not understand...

Am I living my professional purpose? Yes ____ No ____
If no, this is because I do not understand...

If you have a new path in mind such as changing careers, then you can ask the following questions for clarity:
Am I passionate about this?
Will this challenge me to become more?
Can I express my Soul in this relationship or work?
Is this is something that I will enjoy?

Writing Your Destiny Declarations
To make a *declaration* is to state clearly in formal terms, or to officially announce, to yourself and the world what you are about to do. For example, we might declare our love for someone or declare a major in college. I invite you to declare yourself as *the Chosen One for your Destiny*. You do not have to wait for fate, or have any outside force

declare you as *the One*. You have already been called by the Divine and you possess incredible gifts and powers that can be used for good.

Perhaps the most powerful two words in our language are *I Am. I Am* reflects the power of your Divinity. Know that whatever words you put after I Am are very powerful, and when you add positive emotion when speaking aloud, your results are amplified even more. Claim: *"I Am the Chosen One for this Destiny. I am worthy of dedicating my life to discovering my Soul's Purpose."*

Having done this, you are now ready to write your Destiny Declarations. It may help to know that the essence of your True Purpose tends to remain the same throughout your life, even though you may change the wording or phraseology. Your *Personal* Destiny Declaration is about who you want to be in the world and with others. Your *Professional* Destiny Declaration is about what you feel passionate about providing to the world and/or what you want to share with others. Both should be a sentence in length and clearly communicate to others what you want to be and do during your life.

To get on purpose in your relationships, you may find it useful to do the inner work to clear the mental and emotional programs you have formed over the course of your lifetime. Ask, *"What is essential to my Soul in my relationships?"*

To get on purpose in your work, incorporate meaning, creativity and congruency into your mission and let go of the limitation that it is any one thing or role. Ask, *"What is essential to my Soul in work?"*

Declaration Guidelines:

~ Avoid using flowery language. I have seen people over-do the wording or go on and on about their Purpose. If you have too many words it is an indication that you don't have clarity quite yet.

~ Avoid getting caught up in high-minded ideas of some big Purpose in life. It is okay to feel a big sense of Purpose, just remember that the more direct and simple that you say it, the more true it is likely to be.

~ A good rule of thumb is that your declarations should fit on a business card, preferably with seven words or less.

~ Let your Soul guide your brainstorming process, because when you receive the perfect combination of words, you will feel the resonant energy of it.

To write effectively, you must have the clarity that comes from really thinking about who you are and why you are here. Without clarity of Purpose, it is very easy to get pulled into the detours of seductive false Purposes. As we discussed before, *False Purposes* are constructed by the ego and involve effort, exertion, and imitation. *False Purposes* may give you visible material results and yet leave you feeling empty, like something important is missing. They keep you in pursuit of the next big thing and have you feeling that are not good enough or that you are supposed to be somewhere else doing something else. This is why it is essential to choose words that will uplift and connect you with your Soul. When you read your declarations, you will feel, *"Yes, this is who I am."*

Sample words for your Personal Destiny Declaration:

Acknowledge	Aspiring	Balance	Beauty
Caring	Create	Courageous	Daring
Different	Empower	Fundamentalists	Fulfilled
Generous	Giving	Happy	Inspiring
Joyful	Loving	Nurturing	Playful
Reassuring	Supportive	Tender	Unique

Sample words for your Professional Destiny Declaration:

Advance	Advise	Affirm	Choose
Compose	Counsel	Create	Coordinate
Develop	Educate	Encourage	Express
Facilitate	Give	Heal	Inspire
Invent	Involve	Lead	Love
Make	Motivate	Organize	Perform
Promote	Raise	Support	Strive
Teach	Touch	Validate	Value
Wisdom	Write		

Examples of Personal Destiny Declarations

You can use Destiny/Soul/True/Divine Purpose interchangeably. Choose words that resonate for you.

"I am a loving and giving human being who values intimacy and demonstrations of loving kindness."

"My True Purpose is to radiate empowerment and freely shine my bright light to the world."

"My personal Divine Purpose is to be of loving service to the people in my life."

"My personal Destiny is to show myself and others how to be more open-hearted and undefended."

"My personal Soul Purpose is to nurture key interpersonal relationships."

"My personal Divine Purpose is to bring people together in unity and harmony."

"My personal Destiny is to use my intuition to help people see where they are blocked."

Examples of Professional Destiny Declarations

"I am a human being who values teaching others to know and love themselves deeply and completely."

"My professional Divine Purpose is to educate and empower people to live with passion, purpose, and possibility."

"My professional Destiny is to inspire people to lead meaningful and extraordinary lives."

"My professional Divine Purpose is to find easier ways to solve technical problems."
"My professional Soul Purpose is to lead people to spiritual enlightenment."

"My professional Destiny is to restore order out of chaos."

"My professional Soul Purpose is to be a master at group dynamics and facilitation."

Journal Entry 9: Declarations

Now that you are aware of your purposes, write a rough draft of your personal and professional Destiny Declarations. Write two versions, the first, is strictly for your use, such as the ones here and second, write ones that are very short and to the point. For example, Master Group Facilitator, Global Awakener, Destroyer of Waste, Beacon of Light. Post them somewhere where you can reflect on them daily. Some people like to put them on their bathroom mirror, or on their computer screen. A key is to move them around every week or so, and change their order as well, otherwise they simply become part of the landscape and you lose your active awareness of them.

Stage Five: Action

"Don't ask yourself what the world needs,
ask yourself what makes you come alive.
And then go do that.
Because what the world needs
are people who have come alive." —Harold Whitman

Stage Five: Action

Action is the fifth stage in the *Destiny Discovery Process*. Without action, knowing your Purpose loses power. There are two detours to watch out for in this stage:

~ holding on when you need to let go of, and

~ letting the need for security or fear dictate your choices when faced with chaos, challenge, or change.

Once you have reached this level of self-knowledge, it is what you do that matters and moves you forward towards the success you desire. **When we chase opportunities instead of creating on purpose, we can lose our connection with our internal compass (heart).** Take note of the distinction between taking action for action's sake and taking *inspired action*. Inspired action comes from the Soul, where you just feel that something is the right thing for you to do.

When you *keep the main thing, the main thing,* you orient yourself around that Purpose, and when you are in your highest consciousness, it does not feel like effort to do what needs to be done to fulfill it. Inspiration just flows from some higher place *through you*, as you are a *Vessel* who channels Divine wisdom.

Humanity's greatest Destiny is to know *Oneness.* As we achieve this level of consciousness, the entire fabric of reality will receive a Divine upgrade because more people will be living their Soul's True Purpose. It's a love affair in a way, because what we do comes from what we love. In romance, a passionate embrace usually leads to the next step in love making, and ultimately to creation. When you finally embrace *who* you are and *what* you are passionate about, you will find that you are, enjoyably, inspired to take action. You will want to "get busy!"

To say we are here to *serve* is to say we are here to *love*. Loving yourself, others, and what you do, causes joy, which is where creation lives. Anything that comes from joy or love *is* worthwhile, whether that be a national campaign to end hunger, feeding the hungry at a local shelter, or simply being the cook within your own home. While passion is what we *feel*, pursuit is what we *do*. The reason we say, "pursuing a career" is because it takes continuous, preferably conscious, effort.

However, with Purpose, *IT* will take you where you need to go and not the other way around. Just get into the flow and follow your intuition, it will guide you to what to do in perfect timing. There will be always be chaos, changes, and challenges to contend with, so just stay in the energy of allowance, and see these them as stepping stones down your true path in life.

The best way is to learn by doing.....and the best way to create a path is to *walk* it; and then see what you discover along the way. As long as you are taking action when inspired, and facing down your fears and doubts, courage is being cultivated. When you have the courage to put yourself *out there,* with no guarantees; you are living powerfully.

Being conscious of your *personal* and *professional purpose(s)* allows you to set goals, fulfill specific dreams or aspirations, and design the Destiny of your choosing. Personally, you may decide that you no longer want to play the role of victim; and would rather be the heroine or hero.

Most importantly, you have to make significant changes in the way that you perceive and respond to the world. Every day, you are given choice-points where you can go into *default mode* or you can find an access point to the heart. When you fall into an old, familiar pattern, try looking for what feels right, and what you can appreciate, so that you stay in a loving and receptive energy with yourself, others, and the world.

Professionally, you may discover that you are meant to be a fashion designer. You might think, "Great! now I know what I am supposed to do with my life." And then a second later, you might respond with, "Not great. I don't know a thing about fashion design." This is where your commitment is tested; you may have to go back to get more training to do what you really want to do. By taking actions like setting goals or hiring a coach, you are creating energy, the fuel that moves you forward.

Destiny Practice:

Writing your daily or weekly intentions and actions will empower you to stay on track; here is a simple process to keep you accountable. On a sheet of paper, write out the following:

The possibility I am creating for myself is:

Purposeful Action 1:
Purposeful Action 2:
Purposeful Action 3:
Purposeful Action 4:
Purposeful Action 5:

Everyday Enlightenment

I am so excited about being committed, focused, and on Purpose in my daily actions because I know that taking these actions will help propel me to my true Destiny.

I love myself enough to honor my commitments. I find it easy and even fun to do what I need to do.

Getting Back on Your True Path

There will come a time, or two, or ten, when you realize that despite your best efforts, you find yourself off course. Having the ability to get back on track quickly and easily will make your life a lot more fun, not to mention less stressful. To put it simply, *to stay on a path with no meaning denies your Soul.*

When we live out of sync with our Soul, we suffer, and yet, the majority of the population does just that. I invite you to see that changing paths, relationships or locations is not a sign of failure; rather it is a sign of growth and an opportunity to become more of who you are. I invite you to consider that there is nothing wrong with the path that you were on, you have simply outgrown it.

Many times we get off path and hope someone else will come and rescue us, which really means we might be waiting forever for our Destiny to find us. In fact; you are the one you have been waiting for. You were born to set new trends, blaze new trails, and shine your bright light. And yes, leaving the path you have known behind is an essential part of your *Destiny Discovery Process*. One of the things I often say to my clients is that "soul growth occurs outside the city of your comfort," which is quite true, and often easier *said* than *done*. You have to get out there on the dance floor of life if you want to discover your Destiny.

I have received numerous opportunities to practice what I teach many times in my life. I remember a few years ago when I was walking along the beach of Padre Island, Texas, where I had lived happily and comfortably for a record eight years in one place. I was contemplating making a move, and the quote came to me: *"You can't discover new oceans unless you have* the *courage to leave the shore."* I had heard this before, but it struck me with its truth in that moment. I knew my Destiny was calling me out of my city of comfort into the unknown. My own coach had said those very words to me during one our sessions, "Your Destiny is in Austin." I sort of knew it, but it also scared me. I knew the comfort of island living, but I also knew if I moved to a bigger city, I would have to step up my game.

Within two months, my life looked like a tornado as I made the move from the beach to Austin. In one year, I packed and moved all of my belongings several times. I also lost a property to the bank, and my rental home was robbed. On the personal side, I was in three significant relationships, became homeless for a couple of weeks (my dog and I stayed with a friend), all while I was building my business. Suffice it to say, there was a lot going all at once and I felt lost, not knowing which way to go. I was scared and in *survival mode* and could not imagine something good coming from all the drama. I felt pounded by the waves of change, and yet, I held tight to my personal vision of having my life work at a higher level.

Ironically, it was because of these over-whelming changes that I learned what mattered most to me. Everything was moving so fast that I barely had time to over-analyze, I just had to trust my instincts. Most importantly, I had to re-organize myself so that I could receive new blessings. And once that internal shift was made within, like magic, the chaos gave way to clarity.

During this time, I met and became engaged to my soul mate, and we created a happy home life in yet another city, though we met in Austin—remember that *clue* from my mentor about my Destiny being there? I am so glad I did not listen to my limited-self and took the risk to venture beyond my city of comfort. During the journey, I lost many *things* that I thought were important (some quite precious like my grandmother's jewelry), but I gained happiness and the kind of security that cannot be taken away by external circumstance.

As I have learned several times in my life, every cycle of change is about self-discovery. Changes and challenges are ideal opportunities to learn about who we are and what we are made of. This happens when we pause, self-reflect, and integrate the past and allow ourselves to grow a little (or in some cases a lot) more. Remember that you already have within you everything you need to create your greatest life. Just tap into your inner wisdom and honor who you really are, believe in the vision that you have in your heart, and you will soon see it in your reality. I promise that when you let go of the nice, but limited, plan that you have for your life, you will step into Destiny's plan.

And when you trust that you are being guided, that you are never alone, and you'll always have support, especially when making life changes, you will succeed *on Purpose*.

These words from meditation teacher Pema Chodren, may bring some comfort if, and when, you are going through your own release process. *"Things falling apart is a kind of testing and also a kind of healing. We think that the point is to pass the test or to overcome the problem, but the truth is that things don't really get solved. They come together and they fall apart. Then they come together again and fall apart again. It's just like that. The healing comes from letting there be room for all of this to happen: room for grief, for relief, for misery, for joy."*

Let me give you another example from a previous client, Melissa who had been struggling for years, suffering from what I call "job dread." She kept thinking that she would find what she was looking for in the "next position." She gave me permission to share one of her coaching assignments with you. I think many of you will resonate with her story of transformation.

How could someone who describes herself as self-motivated and ambitious become neither? Was something wrong with me or was I just off-course? So here I am, a forty something who's done everything "correctly" and well on my way to corporate success, suddenly faced with the fact that I'm not sure I like what this so-called success is. And I've realized that—surprise—there's nothing at the top of the ladder anyway!

The defining point came after I took a new position in a different company that offered what I thought I wanted: more money and more advancement opportunity. But within four months, I was feeling exactly how I felt in my previous position. I was frustrated with the same routine issues that just didn't matter to me; I was unmotivated, uninspired, and unable to fathom how I could go through these motions for the rest of my working life. I had to do something drastic to change my direction because I knew I didn't like where I was heading and subtle changes in direction only led me back to the same situation.

I started working with a career coach to help me tackle the questions of what else can I do and how can I be sure I won't keep getting stuck like this. It was a breath of fresh air getting an outside perspective on this self-imposed bubble to help me realize I could expand the bubble, or even pop it and make a new one. I realized it is better to not have your life all planned out and limit yourself to something you thought sounded good at age 22. Life's journey is not a straight path, even though, as a rule, I'm a planner by nature, I tried to make it one. It was a challenge for me to get that there is no map, no best way to go, no pot at the end of the rainbow when you get to wherever you think you are going. It was time to let the adventurer side of me out!

When I considered what would make me feel alive, happy, I became very clear that living a "dual personality" of enduring work so I could enjoy my life on the weekends just would not satisfy my soul anymore. I came to believe that both of my *selves* could become one and I could actually love my work and my lifestyle. Once I embraced that, it became too hard to deny myself the power to make a new reality. It was a huge mind shift to realize that no one was stopping me. It's ironic how the simplest concepts that everyone knows intuitively are sometimes the hardest to grasp.

This is a wonderful illustration of how Melissa started to awaken to her personal power and make choices aligned with her True Self. Soon after, she started down the path of being successfully self-employed.

One of our greatest challenges is being happy. What prevents most of us from finding and creating happiness is accepting substitutes for the real thing. So the first thing we must do is sort the trash from the treasure of our lives. And then we have to let go of what we thought would make us happy and actually align with *being happy*. Happiness requires that we give up on our worldly attachment to things and false identifications, to step into the *now* moment with appreciation and awe. We also must go beyond our *false self* and be our *True Self* by following our purposeful path in life. Now, let's look at the stepping stones that lead to your Destiny: *chaos, change, challenge, and choice.*

The Chaos Stepping Stone

Nietzsche once said, *"One must still have chaos in oneself to be able to give birth to a dancing star."* What does this mean? And more importantly, why would you want to *dance* with the chaos in your life? You see, without chaos and change, you would never venture out into new territories and discover what you are truly made of, and this keeps life interesting and moving forward.

The new science of chaos theory teaches that chaos is actually a creative force for change and a "prelude to metamorphosis." Consider how a caterpillar emerges from its cocoon of comfort, and you may see the connection between chaos and finding your Soul path. After growing in strength through the struggle of breaking through its protective barrier, the caterpillar finally transforms into a beautiful butterfly. It needed those moments of discomfort and chaos to not only grow wings, but to appreciate its ability to fly free.

Chaos is about the ongoing process of creation that occurs when thoughts, feelings, particles, and magnetic fields collide, interact, and form into new shapes and concepts. Basically what *was* gives way to 'what is.' When this happens in your own life, it can knock you off-center and create a great deal of fear and uncertainty. So what is there to do?

For inspiration, we can look to nature and how she handles chaos. Nature abounds with creative self-organizing systems that seem chaotic and destructive, but are actually life-giving. Volcanoes erupt to create new landmasses, ocean waves beat upon rocks and beaches to carve out a new shoreline, wind and rain formed the Grand Canyon. Everything on the planet is giving way to the new energy as Mother Earth herself is evolving. Human beings are bound to get caught up in the tidal wave of shifts in thinking and ways of being that come from knowing more of our truth.

When we allow chaos to do as she will, and tune in to our higher consciousness; we greet life's changes and challenges, as personal growth opportunities. When we mature in our thinking, we see triggering events as signs of where we can still use some healing, where we can expand in our abilities, or grow in wisdom.

The symbol for *crisis* written in Chinese is a combination of the symbols for *danger* and *opportunity*. We sit right in the middle of such a moment in human history, where so much is changing that you may feel as if you are losing your mind. *Aha!* Now you are onto something. Our Divine nature calls us to shift from our head to our hearts and is asking us to start living from that place.

When things get messy and chaotic in our own lives, we can be sure that we are being given a divine sign that it is time to correct the course we are on. And when we walk through the *fires* of our own *hell* we can usher in a new reality, one that is more in alignment with our Divinity. When we respond, not react, to chaos from the power of our Soul, then things do not seem so bleak or scary. We begin to find faith.

Since our divine calling is to know ourselves and create happiness, we must see past so-called appearances and not be seduced by socially acceptable ways of being or living. Chaos is a major clue that our life is about to take a turn for the better. Isn't that nice to know?

Everyday Enlightenment

It is when chaos is present, that possibility is created.

The Change Stepping Stone

The cliché, "the only thing we can count on is change" is true. Yet many people resist change, especially when it crashes over us wave after wave. When we step into our Purpose, *there are waves* of change, but instead of retreating back to the shoreline, we can simply learn how to surf. There are two kinds of change: *voluntary* and *involuntary*. Those who desire to be successful in the modern world assess what changes are on the horizon and plan ahead to make them before they have to be made *the hard way*. They understand that *voluntary change* is easier and feels more empowering. So if you want to make a quantum leap on your path, initiate a ton of changes and do things opposite of the way the "old you" would.

Start changing everything to initiate change in your life, from the way you part your hair to where you get your coffee to how you sign your emails. Yes, even tiny little changes like these will open you up to learning how to embrace the change you are wanting. Be forewarned, however, that you will have to tame your inner mental monsters first, otherwise instigating too much change can trigger all kinds of difficult reactions and events that you are simply not ready for until those inner mental monsters are under control.

We are biologically wired to resist change and often wait too long to get on board with the Soul's program. If you drag your feet, eventually, the Universe will force your hand. For example, many people have become dis-heartened in their career. They know they need to move on but are unwilling to take the leap of faith. Often, these same people will get downsized or terminated from a position and then have a hard time re-calibrating to create something new—this is an example of when you have been given the signs, you have ignored them, and as a result, the Universe was required to hit you over the head with a two-by-four.

When you hold on too long and the Universe takes the decision away from you, you tend to continue to look longingly at the door that has closed behind you, rather than seeing the many new doors that have flung open right in front of you.

As you can imagine, *involuntary change* is rampant when the entire structure of society is breaking down. Downsizing, economic insecurity, and natural disasters are necessary ingredients to dissolve everything that has been built from ego and illusion. A powerful metaphor is to imagine yourself with a surfboard on a Hawaiian beach. The waves are huge and magnificent and you have the choice to either climb onto your surfboard (even if you only lay on it) and ride with the waves, or to stand there holding your surfboard upright in the sand trying to stand against them. Which option will you choose?

In any situation you are in, you have four choices: accept it, change it, remove yourself from it, or get support to handle it. There is nothing to fear about change, in fact; it is what makes life a great adventure. When you are a visionary who is on purpose, you will thrive during any conditions, especially challenging ones. One of the key components of the shift of consciousness we are in, is the ability to recognize *Illusion* from *Truth*; and to realize that our perception affects what we see, think and feel. As you master the art of change, you begin to use change as the *golden key* that opens the door to Destiny.

Become a Master of Change

When you are open to change, you more easily welcome new opportunities, people, and resources that will bring you closer to the Divine and allow you to express your highest potential and Purpose. So how do you know when it is time for a life change? Your first clue is when you are resisting something. Resistance is usually a clear sign you are headed in the right direction. For example, you may have resisted leaving a job that you have outgrown even though you knew your heart just was not in it anymore. This is a painful way to live because your Soul knows there is something more for you. Being aware of when you are in (and out) of alignment with your True Self will provide most of what you need for this journey to your Destiny.

Keep in mind that you are either stretching or stagnating, so learn to become attuned to the nudges from the Universe, and be responsive when asked to make changes to let go of what you have outgrown. When it is time to move on from a job, relationship or attitude, embrace the change and be gentle with yourself as you make the transition.

Have you ever noticed how freeing it feels when we make an empowering change? What helps to manage, even embrace change is to remain open and receptive in your heart. Practice being grateful for all that life brings; appreciate what you have in your life, even the messes or stresses, then you grow in your spiritual maturity.

When you can make peace with your life story, and come to understand how you actually chose all of it, you can begin to take 100%

responsibility for knowing and honoring yourself in a way that accelerates your growth. I certainly did this in the midst of my personal turmoil. I was thankful for what was working and prayed to be shown what I needed to see so that I could move forward. I asked to be given the capacity to handle what was happening with strength and ease—to be the kind of person who could trust myself and the Universe, despite appearances.

Also bear in mind, as your world gets turned upside down, what is needed is not merely change, but transformation. Change may mean just changing your residence or place of work but that could lead to finding out YOU are still the same, and without a change within, you are fated to recreate similar circumstances.

Transformation requires a leap in your consciousness and absolute trust that you are creating a *new you*. It is the process of shedding the old to prepare for the new, just as the serpent sheds its skin. There is no greater gift you can give yourself than the time and space to look within to find the insights needed to know yourself as a powerful change agent.

Everyday Enlightenment

Every aspect of your Soul wants to express its greatness and is waiting for you to answer the call for change. Can you hear it right now? What within you is ready to move on?

The Challenge Stepping Stone

Too many people let their fear and doubt make their decisions in life, and end up settling for less than their heart's true desires. When a challenge arises, they either give a half-hearted attempt at overcoming it or give up right away—and they are missing a major opportunity for growth and development. What if Oprah had let her childhood abuse define her as wounded and unworthy? Do you think she would have been able to build a billion dollar media empire and become the leader that she is? It's highly unlikely. Instead of letting life keep her down, she chose to use her challenges in life to fuel her unique brilliance. She even publicly shared her battle with weight and sexual abuse, knowing that by being vulnerable, she could help others who might be experiencing the same thing. Oprah is also a great model for what I call "soul success" because she remained true to herself.

There really is no difference between Oprah and you except that she chooses to access higher consciousness, and chooses to live her life on purpose. I am sure you have had "challenges" in life and I am willing to bet these same challenges have made you the person you are today, even wiser and stronger, at least once you learned your lesson. Guess what else...those same challenging moments served a Purpose! They are often *clues* to what your Purpose is.

When a defining moment comes along, you have two options: let it define you or *you define it.* Defining moments usually impact your life and often take you in unexpected directions, ask you to take a risk, or to choose a non-traditional path. I like to call it *Accidental Destiny*—of course there is nothing accidental about it. Keep in mind, they are an important part of our *story,* and we become weakened when we let defining moments define us and strengthened when we, instead, choose to define those same moments.

Defining moments can look like losing a job, going through divorce, or experiencing a health or wealth crisis. Think about one of your own defining moments and see what clue this might have for you in helping you understand where you are meant to go. Consider what wisdom you gained as a result of going through what you did. What are you now aware of that were not aware of before?

Especially when going through a challenge, it helps to have support and guidance on the best way to move through it. However, stubbornness (ego) prevents intelligent people from reaching out for support. However, all successful people in the world know the true secret is the power of mentoring. I cannot express to you the importance of reaching out for the support that you need—having the expertise of a guide who has the map and knows the way to where you want to go is priceless.

Personal transformation comes gracefully when we form a close, intimate connection with a mentor that we trust. That kind of relationship creates the space for us to bare our souls and feel seen, heard, and valued. Human beings are social creatures and we learn by modeling others and being taught what works. Ask anyone who has made it big in life and they are likely to attribute it to at least one mentor that believed in them and showed them a way to succeed. The original meaning of the word 'mentor' is "highest advisor." Each mentor or guide comes bearing a Divine gift that can help you be more of the true you. Personally, I have worked with many coaches, healers, mentors and energy alignment experts. In the story that I shared earlier where my own life felt like a train wreck (as well as many other times including during the writing of this book), I surrounded myself with training programs and professional mentors so that I could move through the transition more quickly and with greater ease.

If I had tried to do it alone, I am sure I would still be struggling and suffering. If I had thrown in the towel, this book may not have ever been written, let alone published.

I think that by now you see that you are unlimited in your ability to form your reality by each thought you think, emotion you feel, belief you construct, and choice you make. To move through any challenge with ease, balance yourself by knowing when to act and when to go into the stillness, this is the "dance of Destiny."

By the way, the only thing you need to know to dance with Destiny during times of challenge is the *next step*. Keep in mind that does not mean having the whole picture painted before you take that step, don't worry if you can't see the entire staircase.

Even though you may have a vision of what you want, stay open to things starting to look differently. Allow yourself to be in communication with your Soul and ask to be shown the *next* best step. And most importantly, during a challenging time, give yourself patience, space, positive energy, and find yourself a professional coach; these ingredients are what I call "Miracle Grow for the Soul."

A client of mine, Rhonda was having a challenge with answering the call of her Soul. Whenever she would open the door to have a look at the life that was waiting for her, she would get terrified at all the greatness that she saw. Who would she be if she had everything she wanted, anyway? We become quite identified with the struggle and stress and may find it hard to imagine life any other way.

As Rhonda said, *"Destiny is a big scary word to me. And yet the pain of ignoring my inner drive to fulfill my Destiny is still there, I have seen what it looks like and that is the scariest things of all."* She learned to take action that helped her to face the changes and challenges that were calling her forth and you can too.

By the way, when you don't know what to do, that is when the real journey begins, because it is where your internal guidance system takes the lead, and you simply create the *space* for changes. Often we get in our own way by over-doing, over-analyzing, and subconsciously blocking what wants to happen. There must be space for your Purpose to show up and that involves letting go of the life you have known to step into the great *unknown*.

Fortunately, when you make that all important *first step*, Destiny comes running to meet you in the form of support and synchronicities that line up a completely new and bright reality.

Everyday Enlightenment

When a defining moment comes along, YOU define it.

The Choice Stepping Stone

The strongest principle of success lies in our free-will, known more commonly as choice. Our choices and decisions weave the fabric of our lives. As the great self-help writer, Og Mandino said, *"When we were given dominion over the world, we were also given dominion over ourselves. God is not our navigator. It was never his intention to chart a course for each of us and thus place us under his bondage. Instead, he bestowed each of us with intellect, talent, and vision to map our own way, to write our own book of life in any manner that we choose."*

Every choice you make in life either moves you toward your Destiny or away from it. To that end, the wiser your choices, the happier and more successful you are destined to be.

We choose on different levels: individually and collectively, consciously and subconsciously, superficially, and from the depths of our Soul. Most importantly, we choose the meaning that we assign to our life experiences. And as soon as we define something as "acceptable or not acceptable" we are making meaning of it, therein creating the story of it. Ideally, we want to be as conscious and soulful in our choices as humanly possible, aligning ourselves with our Purpose, priorities, vision, and values.

Choice moves you from stagnation into action, from uncertainty into direction, and there is nothing inherently good or bad, in them. Choices simply move us forward in life or not. Choice really is your *super power;* because when you powerfully choose something or someone to be in your life, you are literally carving a path for yourself. The important thing to see is that you can never accidentally remove something that is meant to be on your path. If it is meant to be there, it will come back. If it is no longer aligned with who you are and where you are going, then it will fall away.

My client Anna, for example, was in an unhappy marriage and waited five years before she filed for divorce. When she finally made this major life decision, the fresh energy and her new open attitude magnetized many new friends, she lost excess weight, and even got a promotion at work. Her life literally opened up before her eyes. She became impassioned with a new sense of Purpose and came to see that her first husband was a critical piece to her own evolution. Anna pushed past her comfort zone and stepped into her courage zone, which is where Purpose and Destiny live.

When is it time to Change?

When thinking about making changes, the part of us that is designed to keep us in our comfort zone, the saboteur, gets hyper-vigilant—it's like having your foot on the gas and the brake at the same time-you don't go anywhere. Remember, you cannot become what you want by remaining what you are. When you outgrow a path and choose to move on, your persona may have its ego crushed momentarily, and you may go into crisis mode.

However, I promise that when you look deeper, you will see that a crisis is really just the sudden awareness that you had been buying into an illusion. You are better off without the thing, job, or relationship that you thought you needed. Surrendering is one of the greatest skills required during your journey, yet it makes space for what is truly meant for us.

Some common motivations for choice-making are survival (*Victim*), opportunity (*Victor*), self-esteem (*Vehicle*), and inspiration (*Vessel*). In *Vessel* consciousness, you have become a clear channel, without resistance, resignation, and the critical voices in your head sending you in circles. Instead, you can choose to tune in to the still small voice that says, *"This way to Destiny."*

When we hold on, rather than letting go, we are squandering our power of choice. A good rule of thumb is that if something doesn't feel good or perpetually irritates us, then something needs to change. That is what these stepping stones are for, to teach us when to move on. Making poor choices is one of the main reasons we miss our Destiny in life. To heal this, we must go through an alchemical process of transmuting our reactive self into a present and 'at choice' human being.

To make more conscious choices we need three things:
Acceptance is peacefully being with what is.
Power is the wisdom to know that by changing our mind and hearts, we can change our life.
Presence is the invitation to allow grace to guide our life.

The Soul's liberation that we are all searching for is created by our conscious choices. Those two words "conscious and choice" say it all. To be conscious, we are free from our conditioned state of mind and fully present in the now. Freedom comes when our limited selves stop trying to take the wheel of our life and we surrender to our Soul. Thus, learning to cope with stress and having daily practices that bring us back into balance is an essential life skill. As we evolve in our human consciousness, fear loosens its grip, courage becomes our greatest ally, we take bigger risks, receive more support, and make more spiritually smart choices.

The more spiritually smart we become, the easier our path seems to be. The level of consciousness that comes with living from your heart is the master key to Destiny Creation, remember the two questions: *Does this path have heart? And, can I give my heart to this path?* Use these questions whenever an important decision needs to be made.

It's been said that choice is Destiny's playmate and I agree. When choosing, be light and playful about it, because when you play with anything, especially options, you are having fun.

Remember that if you choose something and it does not work out, you can simply choose again. Always remember, you cannot foul up your Destiny (well, not too badly anyway), but you can certainly delay its arrival. And who wants to wait another lifetime anyway? With crossing the stepping stones of change, challenge, and choices, you can do it right this time around – you can own your Destiny right now!

Journal Entry 10: Choice

Think about a decision that needs to be made in your life.
Feel what you feel in your body. Notice the feelings and write them down.

Ask yourself, Will it pay off? Will this be rewarding?
What is the worst case scenario? What is the best case scenario?
Choose a course of action and then list 3 specific steps you can take to support your choice.

Self-Coaching Exercise:
Making Spiritually Smart Decisions

Ask yourself: Is this coming from my ego or Soul?
Does this feel right for me?
Will this be rewarding for me?
What does my intuition say about this?
Is this my Yes, Yes, Yes?
What signs do I see that support this choice?
Does this move me toward my Destiny?

Stage Six: Allowance

"If we face in the right direction, all we have to do is keep walking." —Buddhist Teaching

Stage Six: Allowance

Allowance is the sixth stage in the *Destiny Discovery Process* and even though it is listed last, *Allowance* is happening at every step of your journey. It is perhaps the ultimate self-mastery skill, one that truly gives you the liberation your Soul longs for. There are two detours to watch out for in this stage:

~relying on your own will instead of following Divine Will, and
~trying to push and force your way to success.

Allowance is a wise state of being that comes from knowing that you are resilient and limitless in your ability to create anew. When you are in allowance, you know and trust yourself at a deep level and easily dance with the stepping stones of Destiny. You have cultivated the courage and vulnerability to let life in, without fear of loss or ruin. You simply (yet powerfully) live with an open and receptive heart.

Your Life, then becomes as great as you *allow* it to be. When you allow your personal journey to unfold in its own uniqueness, with its trials and tribulations, successes and set-backs, you are well on your way to peace and happiness. *Allowance* opens the door to infinite possibilities, where your highest Destiny lives.

The spaciousness of an allowing human being is indeed rare and beautiful. Think of some of the best teachers or people in your life—they just let you be You, right? This same energy can be the way we live, work, and experience our being. And with allowance, all the mental monsters of resistance, resignation, fear and doubt simply don't stand a chance.

The same spacious energy is vital at each stage, whether you are *Awakening*, raising your *Awareness*, stepping into *Acceptance*, *Articulating* your Purpose, or taking *Action* to bring it all together. Allow, Allow, Allow and then *Allow* some more.

The consciousness of allowance brings you an awareness and alignment with Oneness. Knowing yourself as one with the Divine gives you access to higher consciousness by asking powerful questions of your highest self. And learning to live in *Alignment with the Divine* is what the *Allowance* stage is all about. It is where you are open, positive and receptive to Divine Guidance.

Destiny Practice:
I am the allowance for my greatness, love, success, and abundance.

Following Higher Guidance

Edwin Chapman once said, "*A true man never frets about his place in the world, but just slides into it by the gravitation of his nature, and swings there as easily as a star.*" Your Soul is your essential nature. It has access to the Destiny blueprint that is encoded within you and your Soul will guide you, if you allow it. Further, your Soul Purpose is like a river that pulls you along, so whenever you go against Destiny, you may experience struggle and stress. However, when you leap, with faith, into where you are called to go, you will flow and grow.

Unlike arriving at a specific destination on a trip, you do not come to an end with your Soul Purpose. You don't really "accomplish" your Destiny, for it is truly a journey of a lifetime. You do, however, feel as if you are aligned with it, and learn to allow something greater than yourself to navigate the twists, turns, trials and tribulations. Your life experiences are the very clues required to uncover your reason for being here.

Everything in your experience is the curriculum for your enlightenment and your Soul helps to set the stage for your greatest performance; although you always have free will to either follow or not follow your inner guidance (or not). There is a voice inside of you that draws your towards the Destiny you were made for, and when you follow that voice, you will find the freedom that we keep talking about. As you trust your personal growth process, you know that no matter what is happening, it is serving your *raison d'être*—reason for being.

As you have learned, your Purpose is not limited to what you do. In fact, integrating *being* and *doing* is where you feel the most connected to Source and the most fully alive. It's that connection to Source that allows you to embody your inner brilliance and is reflected in your life choices, thus fulfilling your Destiny. And as you learn to trust your Soul more, you will find it easier to live in the moment and trust that your life is unfolding as it is meant to.

You discover that you will know whatever you need to know, just when you need to know it; all you really have to do is take the next step on your path. In fact, if the path before you is too obvious, then it may not be your highest path. Destiny's path is often more than we can imagine. So, if we saw the whole of it, our limited-self might shut us down.

Remember, resistance is just fear, doubt, and disbelief mixed up into an illusionary barrier that keeps you from opening the door to your Destiny. And you already have the key to open the door! You have been given exactly what you need to mature in your self-understanding, and your courage, faith, and intuition grow as you take each step. With each empowered thought you think and inspired action, the more aligned you become: working, loving and living collaboratively with your personality and your Divinity.

To have a Soul Aligned Personality means living with your Soul in the driver's seat while the ego takes a back seat. You become radiant, like a rare jewel that shimmers. Mere ambition is replaced with the evolutionary impulse to be whole-hearted and useful to others. You stop looking for yourself where you are not, or relying on the "good opinion" of other people to validate yourself. You cultivate a deep relationship with your highest self, which has the insight and answers that you need; a beautiful partnership, based on wholeness and the pursuit of authentic happiness.

When creating the person you want to be and the work you want to do, it is important to pay attention to your longings—this is your Soul communicating its deepest desires. The word *intuition* is Latin for "in to you," and listening to your intuition, you will make wiser decisions. Contrary to popular belief, life is *not* meant to be a struggle. You may struggle and stress through life or you may sing and dance; it really is your choice.

The Divine wants you to dance, but not by yourself, rather, in partnership. What happens when two people try to lead when dancing? It looks and feels clumsy, not to mention that someone usually gets their toes stepped on. This is what happens when we (namely our ego) try to lead when there is something higher that knows the dance steps better than we do. Remember the word Guidance as "God, U and I Dance" and that is exactly what starts happening when you let your Soul be your guide.

Your Soul knows the dance steps. Your Soul knows where you are meant to go, and even the best route to get there. Guidance is when the Divine light within you lights your path, and you intuitively know the next step to take. When you allow yourself to be led, tune into the music, and sing the song in your Soul, you will truly be dancing with Destiny.

How do you know if it is your ego or Soul leading your life? Your ego will keep recreating the same scenarios day after day, insisting you learn the hard way. When it is your Soul leading, there is less-struggle, things fall into place as if by magic, and you become a magnet to your desires.

Do your best to have faith in your process of unfolding. Refrain from becoming attached to how you think it is supposed to look—that is your ego. It has its limits for success, happiness, and love, remember? You may receive a Divine download that you need to take a brand new route or to re-invent how you are doing things. This is all part of the transformation process and is necessary for you to become who you were born to *Be*, so trust it, and listen to your guidance at all times, *especially* when it does not make logical sense. The heart has reasons of its own and is the keeper of your treasure map.

Deciding to Be Successful

Success, on some level or another, is a state of being that every human being strives for. A sense of success follows us from when we are toddlers to when we become grandparents. Yet most of us look for success in external forms and end up feeling like we are missing something until we can reach a certain level of money, love or recognition. The ironic thing is that just as we reach that plateau, we feel compelled to go higher still.

This sense of ever-reaching is part of the human experience. The question is how to handle it with grace? I have found that the best way is by becoming more expanded, more conscious, and more committed; and of course to be perfectly at peace *wherever you are on your path.*

You must learn to expect success from life because you have made the decision to succeed. You simply decide it and then you do it. *Yes, just because you say so.* The Universe says *yes* to what you believe—whether positive or negative, so whatever is in your mind creates the fate of your future. Remember what we have said all along about making conscious what is unconscious, so we can do a Destiny shift from living a default life to one of conscious choice.

We are masters of our own universe and can have, be, or do anything our heart desires. The key is to want to become something more from the reaching and the risking, not for the end result. I think we all would agree that Success does not depend on material things, such as driving a certain car or holding a prestigious title; although those things often look like worldly success.

Success does not come from having a million dollars in the bank, although that does give you more personal freedom. Success does not come from doing important things in the world, although others may tell you so. You cannot feel successful based on anything in the in the external world. In fact, you cannot *feel* anything outside of yourself. You can only *feel successful* in your internal world. In other words, it's how you feel on a day-to-day basis that really matters.

Can you go to bed every night feeling successful? Most cannot. Why? Because they are buying into other people's definitions of success and trying, unsuccessfully, to overlay these definitions on their true self, as if they can force it to be true.

Try my definition on for size and see how it feels to you: success is doing what I say I am going to do when I say I am going to do it. *I decide and then I do.* Sounds easy enough, so why do so many people drop the ball when they commit to themselves? Often, they have not developed those expanded personal qualities that will help them.
For example:

- Successful people have the courage to grow beyond their comfort zones.
- They are whole-hearted and focused, pursuing a grand purpose (as defined by them).
- They are fascinated, not frustrated; curious, not complacent.
- They ask for and are open to receiving coaching and mentoring.
- They are committed to staying awake and aware.
- Successful people are willing to do the inner work necessary to achieve greatness and they are very, very, very persistent.

Consider this, have you ever made a conscious decision to be successful? My guess is no. Here is your official invitation to feel, and be, successful.

Destiny Practice:

I, your name, decide to be successful right now, despite what challenges and obstacles I see. I am doing wonderful work and I am proud of myself for accomplishing this today____________.

Soul Success

This new era of living requires an upgraded concept of success. I call it "Soul Success," which is about living a life of mastery, purpose, and meaning while experiencing joy, happiness, and love on a daily basis. It is approaching life, goals, and success from the inside out and aligning with your values, purpose, and vision. Soul Success is about building your life upon a strong spiritual foundation. Soul Success is working together to help each other's dreams come true.

We now have a new measuring stick for success; instead of money, possessions, or prestige, we measure our success by the level of inner peace and fulfillment that we have.

Success of any kind is a team sport, so I would suggest that you work with coaches and mentors who have mastered knowledge and skills that you will need to succeed. Take a look around....who can support, guide and uplift you? Talk to your success-minded friends and family and ask them to get involved in what you are up to in the world.

Doing the transformational work of being who you were born to be leads you to a life worth living. It's a daily commitment, and that is why there are simple, but daily destiny practices to follow in this book. We must *be in the habit* of staying conscious and aware. The small price you pay for a great life is a *willingness* to follow where your Soul moves you, without the resistance, resignation, fear and doubt that weighed you down before, and a *commitment* to stay the course when the chaos, changes, challenges and choices come your way.

An authentically happy life is where you integrate Purpose in all areas of your life: relationships, career, health, wealth, and lifestyle. You radiate an inner warmth and loving light because you know that all is well with you and your world. And this could be your version of success if you *choose to create it.*

During the journey, be sure to celebrate your successes, big and small by taking a moment to see how far you have come. Even a year ago, it would have been hard for me to imagine where I am today. And I am certain this is because I walked through the fires of my own personal transformation through several major transitions to know and embrace my own greatness.

Know that every step *you* take, every book you read, every shift of consciousness you have, is helping not just you, but others as well—we are here to help each other find our way.

As we move into a higher understanding of *ourselves*, we realize that life is meant to be an enjoyable and adventurous experience. Of course the Destined for Greatness Path will have its challenges, however, you will be well-equipped to handle them, because you *know* that you are being guided every step of the way. You have erased those feelings of being separate or that something is missing and you have consciously aligned with your Divinity.

When you allow love to shine through you, your mind and will are working together with Divine Mind, co-creating your life in the highest and most enjoyable way.

When considering your dreams and goals, never ask yourself if you are *good enough* to do something. Ask yourself, *Will I enjoy it? Can I give my heart to it?*

Enjoyment is the path that leads to fulfillment. You *deserve* to enjoy what you are doing and who you are being in life. One way to experience more enjoyment is to give yourself permission to be creative. Creativity leads to deeper self-understanding, and is also a way to share who you really are with the world. Think out-of-the-box and create the life of your dreams because life itself is your masterpiece.

By creating your life based on your vision, purpose, and passions, you will experience more joy and inner peace. And remember, when you are being and doing things *on Purpose*, others benefit and can learn how to live *on Purpose* too.

All you have to do is *be willing to receive*...when allowance is your way of being, you begin to bloom and open to aspects of yourself you never even imagined. Miracles, opportunities, and support become everyday experiences, making life much easier and a lot more fun.

Blooming on Purpose

Your Purpose fills the empty place that lived in your heart before you embarked on this journey. Emptiness has become filled with meaning, passion, and empowerment, you have a greater ability to love, and that, ultimately, is what humanity's Divine Destiny is all about.

Living out your Soul Purpose involves seeing the meaning in the everyday experiences of life—achieving *everyday enlightenment.* A Zen proverb teaches; *"Before enlightenment, chop wood, carry water. After enlightenment, chop wood, carry water."* Nothing really changes in the outside world, but the inside world is radically renewed; it is loving, open, bright, and allowing.

Now that you have begun to discover that your inner treasure lies within by choosing to live your Destiny, you enjoy higher awareness in your thoughts and actions. You have become mindful of what you are doing as well as the underlying motivations, which may, or may not, move your forward. You let go of anything that is illusionary in favor of living true to your True Self, becoming ever more joyful, alive, and fulfilled.

You may notice a certain grace that was not there before in your heart, as you more deeply connect with other people in your life. You start to notice the "little things" that make life special. You also step with a renewed sense of confidence onto your path of greatness and follow it, no matter where it leads. Your path may lead to being a powerhouse in business, education, technology, healthcare, or it may lead to being more loving and kind to the grocery clerk.

Purpose is expressed in everything you say and do, so you can set your Soul free to roam far and wide in the world, or you can stay close to home. It really does not matter anymore, because when you truly know, honor and love yourself, you are exactly where you are meant to be.

You no longer look outside for something to bring happiness, and all that tension is replaced with relaxation, as you learn to flow in the river of your best life. You simply commit to shining your bright light, which will help to bring about a global change in consciousness.

To experience the enjoyment of a full heart and active mind, all you have to do is stay present, share your presence and happily walk your unique path. It's amazing grace.

As we come to an end of your *Destiny Discovery* journey, ask yourself *"What does Destiny ask of me now?"* Bypass your brain, surrender to your Soul, and let yourself go, because *you* are like a flower, who knows its only duty is to bloom—once you find out what you are meant to be and do, you will start to bloom in unexpected directions.

Your ***life*** is a big, beautiful, blooming flower with numerous specially decorated petals making up your unique experience.

Your ***lessons*** are your personal learning and growth opportunities.

Your ***values*** provide direction and guidance for important life decisions.

Your ***vision*** is your overall blueprint for the kind of life you want to lead.

Your ***purpose*** is who you want to be and what you want to share with others when you are at your absolute best.

Your ***passions*** are the things you love.

Your ***life's work*** are the on-going personal and professional projects that you complete.

Your ***goals*** are mini-steps that help support your work, purpose, and vision.

Your ***roles*** are the parts you play along your journey.

Your ***soul mates*** are those who come into your life to love, lead, or teach you.

Your ***supports*** are the habits and environments that bring you a sense of balance.

Your ***path*** is the way you choose to create your life by the choices you make during your journey.

Your ***Soul*** is the architect of your Destiny and will lead you there if you allow it.

Destiny Discovery is a lifelong process that requires going on a Soul Journey to knowing your Soul's Purpose. Be willing to stay the course, go the distance, and of course, enjoy your *self* along the way.

Epilogue:

Enjoying the Mystery of Life

"We wake, if ever at all, to mystery" says Pulitzer Prize-winning American author, Annie Dillard. The Awakening process is never complete; rather it is continuous, with our main goal to be fully aware in the present moment. As we move along our path, we begin to feel the presence of our Divinity, guiding us. We stop limiting ourselves by thinking we know it all, and simply become receptive and open.

And just like a dance, where there is an invitation to glide from one step to another, we can feel the same about life when we are on Purpose. We can plan and scheme all day long, but more often than not the journey takes us in a different direction than we expected. In fact, we often run into Destiny on the roads we take to avoid it. Just know that we can't really miss our Destiny when we are following higher Guidance.

Our limited self thinks it knows what is best, but it does not have the vision to see the bigger picture. Have you ever noticed that when we *don't get* what we think we want, that it often places us on our true path in life? When we mature enough to view life from a higher perspective, then we get to enjoy more of what life has to offer.

Evolution is the very Purpose of our Soul's journey. So when you surrender "expectations" for expectancy, you become *the space* for authentic happiness. Being happy with what is, while inviting more in, is a high state of alignment, empowering you to remain strong and resolute when chaos, change, and challenge threatens your sense of balance.

The *Destiny Discovery* is about being "happily delighted" with your experiences and giving everything you have to Life itself. You live at full wattage, shining your brightest light for all to see. You are bold in your actions and let go of thinking that you need to have everything all figured out. You just follow your heart.

So who are you and where are you going? Holding these questions in your mind on a regular basis will keep you on course, as who you are today will invariably be different than tomorrow or next year. You will change your ideas, preferences, beliefs, even purposes; and that is the way it is meant to be.

As you come to the end of this journey, you recognize that you are about to begin a new one, hopefully with more insight and personal empowerment. Good for you. I invite you to commit to a continuous process of self-discovery, because that is a rare form of success indeed. Enjoy the mystery of it all, let your Soul lead you, and pay attention to what resonates in your heart. That is all there is. Remember that there is no beginning or end, because the journey of your Soul is infinite, and just like the infinity symbol ∞, everything comes around at just the perfect time, in just the perfect way. You are always protected, guided, and loved, each step of your journey.

As you continue to become a clearer, more open conduit for an awakened consciousness, Divinity shines through you ever more brightly. You will grow in your faith and risk-taking, stepping into your courage zone more often, growing rapidly. To stay the course, it helps to share the journey with trusted friends.

Modern science has proven the efficacy of experiencing *Aha* moments, asking powerful questions, and being supported through your personal growth process. Because we are social beings, we learn the most from our close relationships. As humanity continues to deepen the connection to our Creator, we will also need to stay connected to each other.

The way to purpose and success is to join a community that shares similar values. You may feel that you would like to receive more guidance than a book can provide or that the *Destiny Discovery* process has started a shift in your life and you would like to be supported as you move through the various changes that might result from this kind of personal growth. If this is the case, we encourage you to find a healer, coach, or mentor who can guide you through these changes.

If you do not have access to someone, then visit our main site, www.LiveYourDivineDestiny.com. There you can plug into *Destined For Greatness,* our growing global community. You will also find valuable resources to help facilitate a deepening of your *Destiny Discovery* process in our library of resources and meditations.

The Destiny Discovery is meant to be lived.....

It's been my honor to journey with you, and I'm looking forward to when our paths cross again. Here are some ways we can connect:

Destiny Resources

Sign up to receive your free Destiny gifts and join the community that is Destined for Greatness. Scan QR code or go to http://www.LiveYourDivineDestiny.com

Download free self-discovery meditations & audios. Scan QR code or go to http://www.LiveYourDivineDestiny.com/audio

Receive free audio replays of the Destiny Telesummit with 11 world-class experts. Scan QR code or go to http://www.LiveYourDivineDestiny.com/telesummit

Read one of Michelle's 30+ Destiny books (titles include: *Destined For Love, Writing With the Divine, Get Your Career on the Fast Track, and Breakthrough to Greatness*). Scan QR code or go to http://www.BrightLightCoach.com/success-store

Look for "Bright Michelle" on social media and mention that you are a *Destiny Discovery* fan.

http://www.twitter.com/brightmichelle
http://www.youtube.com/brightmichelle
http://www.facebook.com/brightmichelle333

About Your Destiny Mentor & Author

Michelle L. Casto AKA **Bright Michelle** is a woman on a mission. She sets souls free from their mind-made prisons so they can decide their Destiny and reach their fullest human potential. Throughout her career, this powerhouse of personal transformation has been known as spiritual teacher, author, healer, Guru, Soul Coach, consciousness shifter, Lightworker, and "bright light."

To her, she is simply an awakener, a guiding light to higher consciousness and Destiny. Feeling called from an early age, Michelle has always possessed an insatiable curiosity to know the meaning of life and her role in making the planet a better place to be. Her Quest for this understanding led her to understand that Life itself is the curriculum for her enlightenment. For decades, she has studied with some of the world' greatest Luminaries and is now an expert guide for those seeking to find what their Soul is searching for.

"Bright Michelle" has become well known for her "potent magic" that transforms people into knowing & honoring who they are at a very deep level. Clients consistently report radical changes in their thinking and ways of living that are nothing short of miraculous. Michelle recognizes there is a divine spark within every human being that longs to be fully ignited and expressed. Through her company, ***Everyday Enlightenment,*** she writes, teaches, coaches, and inspires people to co-create an amazing reality in both their life and business.

Michelle is a prolific author and has also written: *Destined For Love: A Step by Step Guide to Attract Your Soul Mate, Get Your Career on the Fast Track, Breakthrough to Greatness, Writing With the Divine,* and several other life success topics. Visit her main site **BrightLightCoach.com** to gain access to more of her divinely inspired products.

The Destiny Success Process (Awake-Shift-Shine-Succeed) is taught to people in groups and individually to build a bridge to their inner self so they can tap into the wisdom of their own Souls. The best way to live *The Destiny Discovery* is to enroll in one of Michelle's mentoring programs.

Destiny Mentoring

Enroll in one of Michelle's Mentoring Programs and experience the magic of working with a Destiny Master. Scan QR code or go to http://www.BrightLightCoach.com/mentoring

"Want help discovering your Destiny? I recommend Michelle Casto to help you dig deeper into who you are and let go of your story of what's been holding you back. She is **one of the most empowering Spiritual Coaches on the planet**."
—Elizabeth Grant, Songwriter and Spiritual Mentor

"Michelle's coaching is like a potent **homeopathic medicine for the soul**–just a small dose and I am good for months!"—Alice Geddes, Teacher

"Michelle Casto showed me the way to my ***true path in life*** and now I feel that ***anything is possible***."—Jim Wallace, Business Executive

Honor the Treasure That You Are.

CPSIA information can be obtained at www.ICGtesting.com
Printed in the USA
BVOW031035211211
278924BV00001B/70/P

9 780967 470498